THE CAUSE
OF LIBERATION
IN THE USSR

Queenship
PUBLISHING COMPANY
Santa Barbara, California

THE CAUSE
OF LIBERATION
IN THE USSR

Rene Laurentin

Translated by
Leslie Schlesinger Turner

Queenship
PUBLISHING COMPANY
Santa Barbara, California

This book originally published in French as "Les chretiens detonateurs des liberations a l'est" in 1991 by O.E.I.L. Paris France.

Copyright C 1993 Queenship Publishing Company

Library of Congress Catalogue No: 93-083222

ISBN: 1-882972-07-4

Contents

Cover

The church in Kolomenskoe, a village near Moscow, would have been witness, slightly before Fatima, to the protection of Our Lady over Russia which had been given up to atheist dictatorship. The following facts are preserved by the local tradition:

Eudoxie Andrianova, a farm woman from Potchinok, heard a mysterious voice in her sleep on February 13, 1917.

"In Kolomenskoe there is a large black icon. The red icon must be established."

After a second vision (February 26), the farm woman went to Kolomenskoe on March 2 and told the priest her mystical dream.

He showed her the icons venerated by the church. But none of them resembled the one in the dream. He then had the basement searched where a larger icon of the Queen of Heaven was found, in the place of honor draped in a cloth of purple, with specter and globe, the Child on her lap. The farm woman recognized her icon which has became itinerant in the monasteries and churches of Moscow. A hymn was composed in honor of the Mother of God, under the blessing of the Patriarch Tikhon. The prophetic dream came to pass in February, the month of the revolution. Eudoxie's visit to the church happened on the day of the abdication of the Tsar, March 2, shortly before his arrest on March 20. Fatima's first apparition occurred on the following May 13.

The event at Kolomenskoe thus became a preface to Fatima and Medjugorje's messages on the future of Russia. According to the tale of Nicholas Likhatchev, this discovery prophetically announced that Mary was becoming an effigy, through the crowned icon in the cloth of purple, of the Tsarina of Russia after the fall of the Tsar.

Forward

THE THREE LINES OF POWER
AND THEIR SECRET EFFICIENCY

The freedom that is spreading in the Eastern countries is a major event in our century, an event both unexpected and universally important.

This occurrence derives from Marxism-Leninism, the most powerful and most prestigious of all secular powers. It has seduced a great number of intellectuals, including Christians and priests. It had replaced the Church as the liberator of the poor, it was said. And the future of this liberation was using science, praxis, the fight of the Marxist class. Some of these intellectuals still have not turned the page, especially among the liberation theologians and in the universities in Latin America, where Marx still holds prestige.

In addition, the USSR was the largest country in the world - 40 times the size of France, twice the size of Brazil, China and the USA. Marxism had grown and tightened the vast empire formed by the tsars. The USSR had preceded the USA in the conquest of space. They had the largest armed forces in the world, the most powerful police force, and the support of a Communist Party in most countries. The Marxist model shone a little bit everywhere. The regime had widely spread in Asia, with more than a billion men, in Africa, and in Latin America where Nicaragua had followed in the steps of Cuba. But those who lived in this paradise loathed the red tape, the lies, the terror, the material and moral misery, the persecutions, the camps, the psychiatric hospitals, without any visible hope of bringing down this iron regime.

However,against all odds, no later than last year, with the sound of the two small words spoken for some time now by Gorbachev, glasnost and perestroika ("opening" and "rebuilding"), the USSR has changed face, spectacular liberations were taking place in the satellite countries of the East. Through democracy, Nicaragua has abandoned the Marxist regime. Castro has found himself alone, criticized, even in Moscow, for his retrograde Stalinism.

A breath of liberation had passed. Dictatorship had given way to democracy; the balance of terror to disarmament; persecuting atheism to religious freedom; Marxist economy to a free market economy. Why?

I do not pretend to speak as a specialist on the USSR, and honestly I must situate the niche wherefrom I speak. I have been studying Marxism since 1935, and I have benefitted from lectures in outstanding analyses by Lallement at the Catholic Institute. I have been following religious events for the past thirty years, with trips in more than 40 countries including eastern bloc countries, with articles and books to show for it. Today I would like to try to place the religious cause, and more specifically, the Christian cause behind these liberations, the reason behind this conference: Liberation of the East, the Churches' Force Behind It (I prefer the word "liberations" to "revolutions",

I do not intend to overemphasize the value of this Christian factor or to make it into an exclusive cause. I only want to declare some facts and astonishing convergences that seem to be unknown to various degrees. Everyone remains the judge of their exact importance and their interpretation on historical as well as religious grounds. I will present a general view of the three following lines of thought:

1. The most obvious and objectively established - the role of Poland.

2. Religious resistance in which Christians have played a significant role.

3. I finally will talk about causes of a mystical nature. I have hesitated to do so and would not have dared to do so if they had not taken shape in a surprising manner, like a societal phenomenon. By this I mean the predictions and fulfillment that progressed from Fatima to Medjugorje.

Book I

Overview

1

The Polish driving force: from the consecration of the three W's to Solidarity's discrediting of worker Marxism

Poland is the country where I best followed these events, in the course of a dozen trips staggered from the end of the sixties to the last few months.

It took me some time to understand this country, which did not have any importance in the media until the onset of the eighties. At the Second Vatican Council, Cardinal Wyszynski, Primate of Poland, belonged to the minority. The majority considered him behind the times. And yet, at the news agency in Rome, as well as in the corridors of the Council, each Pole I met, including leftists, defended without question this man that foreigners gladly called retrograde.

Cardinal Wyszynski had everything against him when he became Archbishop of Gniezno-Varsovie, Primate of Poland, in 1948. The country was coming out of horror (six million dead and ruins). It had gone from Hitler's domination to Communist domination. For centuries, Catholic Poland, for centuries Catholic, had become Nazi; and Orthodox Russia fad become atheistic. From the religious point of view, Poland was then less Catholic than France; its Catholicism had largely become sociological. There were then close to 50,000 priests in France and barely 10,000 in Poland. The shortage of men, of means, of freedom, was tragic.

In 1953, Cardinal Wysznski was imprisoned in a residence under strict surveillance from the Police, cut from all contact with his Church that the government was dividing by establishing associations of priests more or less affiliated with the regime. For this man of action, reduced to idleness, it was enough to induce a breakdown. The Cardinal saved himself by praying and resorting to God alone, but in depth. On December 8, 1953, he gave all to God through Mary, the woman who brought God to the world so that the world would be brought to God. He had prepared himself, by spending three weeks in retreat, for this consecration, according to Saint Louis Marie Grignion de Montfort. Material slave of an anti-religious dictatorship, he was becoming a slave of God through Mary for the purpose of an active liberation. Consequently, he worked without a break on a second project: the consecration of Poland, of which he was the Primate. He planned a rechristianization of his country on all levels: catechism, family, seminary, and episcopate.

On August 26, he was ready. He performed this consecration, or rather had it performed at the Notre-Dame of Czestochowa National Sanctuary. Upon sending the act in secret, he declared

"Let a bishop read this consecration; if there is no bishop, a priest; if there is no priest, a layman, whoever he is, so that it is read."

Unexpectedly, his liberation occurred soon after; miraculously, some said. And he achieved the training program for which he had given himself 10 years, up to the millennium of Poland's Christianity, which he celebrated in 1966. His work was unknown, hindered as it was from all directions. Pius XII reproached him for supporting the extension of Poland towards the West, to the detriment of Germany, in compensation for all the USSR had stolen in the East. Nevertheless, his work towards training and secret resistance deeply and, irresistibly grew. It is during these 10 years that Poland became deeply Catholic, ready to deliberately endure all tests. And the Cardinal resistance , the only voice that dared and could speak, won people over step by step, even the non-Catholics. Many came to attend Mass. "Why?" I asked one of them. "Because it is the only place I can openly protest against the regime that has us in its grip."

During each one of my trips which then started, I admired this faith and this growing unity, but they seemed utopian. The people I was speaking to hoped for a miracle. But what could they do against the steamroller that was keeping them flat? What could David and his sling do against the giants armed with tanks that crushed Budapest and Prague? Poland went through a heroic course between two constant temptations: despair and revolt, Charybdis and Scylla. The great power of this movement was its great realism. Cardinal Wyszynski measured, with each step, how far his words and actions could go without starting an irreversible repression. For many long years, persecuted faith kept its strength and maintained its pressure. It was long, very long.

And then in 1978, a first sign of the expected miracle loomed up against all expectations. This did not happen by chance. It was because living Poland had trained men who could measure up to the problems at hand.

Criticism from the Catholic intelligentsia did not relent for all that; the Polish Church was clerical. It was the retrograde triumph of clericalism in the Church.

And now this clerical Church saw the birth of the most incredible secular movement of the century, the Solidarity led by Lech Walesa, militant since 1970, co-founder of the union journal Robotnik Wybrzeza (April,1978).

Millions of workers dared to ask for their rights. The number of forbidden strikes increased. It was such a force that Gierek resolved to negotiate. Lech Walesa signed, on August 21 1990, with a rosary around his neck, the Gdansk Agreements, which extended to the other hot spots of the country - Szczecin, Jastrzebie.

The official existence of the Independent Solidarity Union was acknowledged. It was confirmed, on November 9 1980, by the Supreme Court. All of the dismissed workers were reinstated; prisoners were freed with the effective recognition of the right to strike and of the right of access to freedom of information. This tolerance dragged Gierek to his fall, as Moscow blamed him. He was incarcerated along with his principal associates in December, 1981.

The worker movement seemed irreversible. It probably instituted the most powerful union in the world, with nearly 9 million members, while the Church was encouraging the creation of a large union of private farmers (May, 1981), despite opposition from the political power.

Faced with these disconcerting events, the government was changed, then changed again. On October 18, 1981, Stanislaw Kania, Gierek's successor, was dismissed and replaced by General Jaruzelski, who held his new post as Number One, the Party Secretary, concurrently with his previously held function as President of the Council and Defense Minister. He carries on with the militarization of the Polish administration and systematically prepared an infallible repression.

On December 13, 1981, at sunrise, he decreed a state of siege. The Solidarity unions were abolished; Lech Walesa was incarcerated all of this without bloodshed or time for a revolt to be triggered.

The rise of Solidarity had seemed irreversible to me, as did all of the great social movements. I was stupefied by the triumph of the authorities. The Marxist system, armed by the military and the police, must have not been opposable. Never had Poland been so tempted to despair and revolt. Many were more ready for death than for patience, but they kept, one more time, to the underground fight for their faith.

Thus, the last triumph of the Communist Party machine became a Pyrrhic victory. The repression of the first worker movement, which had suddenly appeared in the Marxist empire, gave the definite proof that Marxism was not a movement for the liberation of the workers anymore. It was a dictatorship more extreme than any other against the workers. How could it be a proletarian dictatorship if it acted against the proletariat? Marxism was discredited. Its prestige, its motives and its credit were annihilated. This was the coup de grace, but the system was holding on.

Faith stayed strong enough to overcome the permanent temptation to despair and revolt. The Church maintained its line of non-violent action, supported by more than 90% of the Polish people against a well-armed but discredited and overwhelmed Party. In the face of the two state forces, the Party and the military, there were now two others, the Catholic Church and the Solidarity workers.

It is important to emphasize that Solidarity was not a clerical force. Walesa was a layman, a worker. The Union stemmed from his initiative as a worker. He was not remote-controlled by the Church, with which he maintained trusting dialogue. He welcomed in his union any workers, independently of their opinions, including Communists. The so-called clerical Church of Poland had given rise to a perfectly independent secular movement (an ideal the Church rarely obtains, except when it relies on faith alone).

Despite Solidarity's independence, all of the resistance forces shared an inspiration and unity deeply rooted in the same faith.

In Poland the three greatest leaders who have ever lived: Wyszinski, Wojtyla, Walesa.

-Wyszynski had performed the double consecration, and one personal in 1953 and one national in 1956.

-Wojtyla (the current John Paul II) had preceded him. He had performed this same consecration, according to the same Saint Louis-Marie Grignion de Montfort, when he was a conscript worker at the Solvay factory, at the beginning of the forties. And this is the secret of his life.

-Walesa performed this same consecration. At the time of triumph of Solidarity, on October 21, 1980, he went, as the leader of the unions that spontaneously followed him, to the national sanctuary of Czestochowa, where the Cardinal had performed his first consecration. He expressed in his turn, with his own consecration, the consecration of the unions which accompanied him, by making common cause with the Cardinal's act.

Thus the last 8 years of resistance that seemed hopeless had succeeded (1981-1989), through extraordinary stages.

-Walesa was freed. He received the Nobel Prize, through his wife, since he could not leave the country. General Jaruzelski, intelligently weighed the irrepressible rise of a nearly unanimous moral resistance, suspended "the state of war", in 1983 (after dismissing 244 judges and 3400 magistrates in 1982). John Paul II's visits to Poland demonstrated and invigorated the rise of this resistance.

On October 17, 1984, the murder of Father Popielusko shocked the Poland and world opinion. The iniquity of the system was unmasked. Some policemen were tried.

In 1989, everything turned upside down; in 1990, Jaruzelski submitted his resignation. What followed (which is more complex) falls outside the parameters of our present subject matter.

The conclusions of our first report are summed up by the following:

1) Poland's victory of non-violent resistance was exceptionally inspired, moderated and coordinated by the actions of the Church, more specifically by the mystical and charismatic leader that was Cardinal Wyszynski. He did not experience the final triumph since he died on May 28, 1981. Before his death, he participated in three arbitration committees with the government and Solidarity, and asked for the resumption of work at a critical time in order to avoid a new coup in Prague.

2) When I met him, a short time before his death, at the end of October 1980, I asked him the question that burned in my mind in the face of his inconceivable success: "After having everything stacked against you, how did you rally everybody, even the government and leftists who turn to you?" His answer was not long in coming. It can be said in one surprising phrase: "But it was the Blessed Virgin!" And, so saying, he showed me the Treatise of Louis-Marie Grignion of Monfort, which was located on his prayer stool. His tone and his glance, firm and sober, expressed volumes. Those who can not accept this will at least recognize, on a more controllable historical and sociological basis, that this Christian resistance was victorious.

3) And it is important to emphasize this because some are mistaken about it. The resistance from the Polish Church was not a political resistance. The Cardinal always placed himself on human, moral and religious grounds, inspired by faith alone, with a deliberate apolitical attitude. It is the rigor of this position that allowed him to subsist; his Christian action gained political weight because he was apolitical. This is the "Golden Rule" for the real successes of the Church.

4) Poland truly was the driving force behind the failure of the Communist system, and that established new ways. The Polish victory led the satellite countries, and this movement has greatly spread in the Russian Empire.

Two more difficult factors are now left to be discussed:

-The Christian resistance

-A mystical aspect of the problem.

2

The Christian resistance

The resistance against Marxist materialism was, in varying degrees, almost everywhere in the Russian empire (not to mention 50 million Moslems and 4 million Jews more locally surrounded) a Christian resistance. The resistance was comprised of 60 million Russian Orthodox, 12 million Catholics, 10 million Protestants in the USSR, and a larger number in the satellite countries.

The Orthodox Church, embarrassed by its substantial official position, had to collaborate with this iron regime in order to maintain its existence, its admirable liturgy and its profound inspiration that brought forth, among its members, hidden and open rebels of the utmost importance: Priests - Doudko, Men (murdered) - Yakounine and the colossal Soljenitsine.

Protestants played an incendiary role in Romania where the Pastor of Timisoara triggered the decisive revolt. They have also sustained a role on the front line in West Germany. Catholics, reduced to an underground existence in the USSR, and tolerated in other places under all sorts of restrictions, did not have a determining role in Polish government. The Ostpolitik was forced to go along with a limited collaboration. It left many episcopal seats vacant, and filled others with candidates who often were mediocre, as opposed to Poland where Cardinal Wyszynski managed it because he had obtained the right from Pius XII to nominate his own bishops.

Eastern Catholics (Greek-Catholics) were most affected. They really had all the cards stacked against them. They were the black sheep of the Communist power that was afraid of their independence. The Orthodox considered these "Uniats" as defectors, unduly united with Rome. And Rome was embarrassed by these eastern Catholics who interfered with the ecumenical dialogue in which their presence would have irritated the Orthodox Christians. They had to be shamefully hidden. Thus they were the most persecuted, the least supported-and the most heroic. I have met these witnesses of the faith, and it was distressing.

In the USSR, Stalin eliminated the Ukrainian Greek-Catholic Church and handed it over to the Orthodox Church who became executor of the arrangement. Many, whatever rank they held, were imprisoned and died, from bishops to the lay people. Deprived of their Church, they performed Mass in the woods. I heard the fascinating testimony of one of them: Josyp Tereyla, imprisoned for 23 years, freed on February 5, 1987, but exiled on September 18th by perestroika in which he did not believe: a man but a witness of the faith.

In Romania, 6 Greek-Catholic bishops were imprisoned, after them 6 more, consecrated in secret by the Papal Nuncio 7 died in prison, two when they were released, another is still very ill; two are still able-bodied. Each one of them was tortured, starved, quartered with intolerable cruelty and invited to occupy a position of honor if they agreed to join the Orthodox Church. None of them gave up. Hundreds of priests and thousands of lay people met with the same fate.

Most certainly, the opposition to the system that was crushing most into passivity was not solely been Christian. In Russia, for example, Sakharov was an agnostic rebel. His admirable and prestigious victory was both scientific and moral, not Christian. Nevertheless, he insisted on getting an audience with John Paul II. Christianity was important to him as a prime force of resistance, and some said (which I could not verify) that his last days brought him closer to faith.

12

But Solzhenitsyn, the other great Russian figurehead, truly is an ardent Christian. This prophet was able to expose, in the East and the West, the same error, the loss of a sense of God. The Occident making matters worse by compromising with the Communist regime, creator of gulags. Solzhenitsyn had found faith again in the absolute emptiness of these repressive camps. There he found the strength for a laborious and wise opposition against the debasement of the numbered man. His work illustrated what Pius XI had said about Marxism being "intrinsically perverse" this qualifier most Catholics rejected as being outrageous. His work systematically proved it. But they also criticized Western materialism: the golden calf of the economy was the creator of a jungle. This prophet experienced the joy of revolt and the laughter of the emancipated slave. He achieved an enormous psychoanalysis of modern man in the absence of God. He transferred the fear of the victims onto the executioners (Le premier cercle, 1968). Consequently, in the heat of destalinization he got the green light from Khrushchev and the Nobel Prize for Literature (1970), then banishment. He knew how to be simple like a dove and wise like a snake, both a prophet and an inspired tactician, always knowing when to strike. He gave proof that the worst horror can harbor a kind of beauty, holiness, a flowering of martyrs in the absolute asceticism that definitively sets the soul free. Beyond his curses against the West and Communism, his basic conviction is that freedom without religious faith can only degenerate or stray. In a very different way from Lech Walesa, he was also, with his depth and talent, a catalyst - a catalyst who ruined in the world, without polemic, the illusions of Marxist propaganda and, let us not forget, the illusions that undermine capitalism.

The importance of the Christian resistance is difficult to estimate, because of lack of statistics on the number of Christians who were imprisoned, interned, and who died in the camps. Such statistics will remain all the more impossible because the Christian motive was generally hidden under other pretexts.

Several references show the considerable importance of this discreet phenomenon due to its secrecy.

1) The supported resistance of the Christians has caused, since the end of the sixties, a wave of conversions. This movement was the more paradoxical because it happened after more than 40 years of solely atheistic teaching. This movement, important qualitatively, is impossible to appreciate quantitatively.

The case of "Marie" founder of the Russian feminist movement Marie is significant. She was born Tatiana Goritcheva and was a young philosophy professor, educated in Marxism. Converted to Christianity through yoga, she founded, in 1979, along with companions converted like herself, a very original feminist movement. It was completely different from American feminism. This movement was under the Patronage of Mary, Mother of God, spurned by the Women's Lib. Tatiana saw in these women the perfect example of women's liberation. It was less a matter of liberating them selves from "male chauvinism" than from Marxist materialism which had destroyed the masculinity of men and the femininity of women, by leaving women to the mercy of ruined and often alcoholic men. These women were expelled in 1980. Since then, Tatiana has been constantly testifying. She has been asked to speak about God even on Soviet television, where she is urged to go on, even at the risk of disrupting the program.

This wave of conversions was another catalyst fatal to the powerful Marxist ideology. Its famous "science", taken on by the liberation theologians, declared that Christianity would disappear by itself, according to the historical determinism. The irrepressible survival of Christianity and its irresistible reappearance were another contradiction to this pseudo-science that was only a promotional ideology.

2) Many priests played a close game in preaching God and the Gospel. But the only success they achieved was incarceration or internment in a psychiatric hospital. From this anonymous class only a few names emerge.

Father Alexandre Men had an extraordinary influence resulting in a whole line of converts. He had many secret publication - Biblical and spiritual works enriched by his knowledge of the ancient and modern languages. He had been sent forty kilometers from Moscow, which did not keep his parish from extending to over 2000 people. In the seventies, his phone was tapped, his parish checked. After the arrest of Father Dimitri Doudko and Father Gleb Yakounine, he was harassed and interrogated along with his parishioners. Glasnost just saved him from being arrested. He took advantage of it to give his action a new public dimension. Every Sunday, he conducted dozens of baptisms; he was impassioned with reversing the enormous ignorance of the Russian people who had been buried in by Marxism. The day before his death, he wrote this optimistic letter to Michel Sollogoub:

"Now, thanks to God, our parish, like many others, has the possibility to develop its activities almost without constraint. We are setting up a library for the young and the children. We have opened a school for adolescents. I now have the permanent opportunity to speak on radio and television. Thank you for what you have given me."

But sadly, this optimism had to take into account the Marxist system that remained in the shadows. On Sunday September 9, at 6:30 p.m., while he was going to his parish, Father Alexandre Men was struck in the back with an axe. He died of his wounds before help arrived.

Father Yakounine who had influenced him, has lived hard years in prison. But he survived. He now is a deputy at the Supreme Soviet. He does not wear his rank insignia, because it contains the Communist hammer and sickle. He remains without compromise, henceforth untouchable at this level.

There would be a lot to say about the influence of the grandmothers, who often transmitted the faith - and baptism, from generation to generation. In every eastern country, the grandmother was a good excuse to justify oneself when the head of the Party learned about a baptism and the head of the family was in trouble:

"It was the grandmother who wanted it. We could not stop her etc."

History will forget their incredible contribution, which is often the role of women to whom is owed the fundamental fabric of the human and religious formation of humanity.

Two other factors are not negligible.

1) Those who were imprisoned in gulags and psychiatric hospitals were successful in transmitting news, but not without risk. Journals such as Christians of the East or Aid to the Faithful of the USSR have bravely distributed them against the current. It took time for them to be heard, but it contributed to the reversing public opinion. Wrongdoing, once exposed, cannot persist for very long.

2) At the time when the system was ruled by fear, the convinced Christians were those who were not afraid. This fearlessness won them the esteem and prestige that are revealed today. It is what gives radiance to the Ukrainian Greek-Catholics, and the convincing power of their testimony (with which the new independent Ukrainian Orthodox Church tries to compete). They serve as leaders of public

opinion and as catalysts for the conversion movement, thousands of baptisms happen with them every Sunday.

In spite of a few dazzling and public cases, it is a capillary phenomenon, but established on various levels, from one end to the other of the Soviet empire and its satellite countries (including China, where the clandestine Church has not decreased, but on the contrary has increased since the beginning of the Maoist Revolution).

A capillary phenomenon is always difficult to evaluate, and I would be grateful if, among you, some have found the criteria to measure it more precisely. It has created a strong fabric, that has undermined the system, and without it changes would have not been possible.

3

The mystical element

I am getting to the third and final element, which I hesitate to talk about, because it only makes sense to those with Faith and will seem utopian to anybody who lacks this gift (unless he attempts to discern in these troubling convergences, either an occult or parapsychological element of unknown causes or a psycho-sociological phenomenon, because its role is not negligible in the evolution of liberations in the East).

Not to overwhelm those who are strangers to this factor, I will briefly expound it. From the late testimony of Lucy, Fatima's seer of the Blessed Virgin told her on July 13, 1917, (thus slightly before the October Revolution):

"I will come to ask of you the consecration of Russia to my Immaculate Heart. The Holy Father will consecrate Russia to me, which will convert itself and the world will know peace for a certain amount of time. In Portugal, the dogma of faith will always be preserved, etc."

This final etc. replaces the famous and last secret of Fatima, the one which has not yet been revealed. But it does not matter for our purposes. On May 29, 1931, Lucy thus wrote the received request:

God asks the Holy Father to perform, in union with all the bishops, the consecration of Russia to my Immaculate heart. He makes the promise to save by this means (text cited by J. ALONSO, in MARIE UNDER THE SYMBOL OF THE HEART, p. 42).

On June 12, 1931, in answer to the question from her confessor, Lucy expresses the same promise more modestly:

God promises to end persecutions in Russia, if the Holy Father deigns and orders the bishops of the Catholic world to perform a solemn and public act of reparation and consecration to the Sacred Hearts of Jesus and Mary.

At this point Lucy specified that the consecration will first apply to the Sacred Heart of Christ (not solely that of the Blessed Virgin: which informs us of the theological or ecumenical objections), and the promise is not about the conversion of Russia anymore but about the end of the persecutions.

Lucy met with a refusal from Pius XI who did not want the Papacy to follow in a private revelation wake. During World War I, four times she obtained the renewal of this conscration from Pius XII, each one gaining another step forward, to be more in conformity with Lucy's request. Paul VI, who was invited to perform this consecration again, limited himself to commemorate it on November 21, 1964.

John Paul II, who had turned down the request for renewal at the beginning of his pontificate, reconsidered it on after the attempted murder that almost ended his life on May 13, 1981. On his hospital bed, he had Lucy's messages read again by Doctor Poltavska. He renewed the consecration on May 13, 1982, the anniversary of the attempted murder, to Our Lady of Fatima herself. But being unable to see Lucy before the declaration of the act, he renewed it twice, more solemnly, on her recommendations, during the Feast of the Annunciation in 1984.

Up to this date, Lucy had always considered that the consecration (already renewed 7 times by Popes) had not been accomplished according to the Blessed Virgin's requests; "Thus it was not done." but after this last renewal, she wrote Mother Belem, "Since this consecration of March 24, 1984, by John Paul II, in association with all of the world's bishops, the consecration is accomplished" (letter from August 9, 1989).

Whatever the nature of all of these texts, which have caused many problems and which were talked about at great length, John Paul II, realizing the powerlessness of his human and diplomatic actions to liberate the churches of the East, again entrusted all to God through Our Lady..

I am aware of how this chain of events is paradoxical. For a long time, Fatima's promise for "the end of persecutions" and the "conversion of Russia" seemed a hardly credible utopia. What could heaven do against earth's powerful system? This promise appeared like one of Fatima's implausible predictions.

Today, the utopia has become credible. In spite of the murder of Father Men, which is like one of the last thrusts from a moribund dragon, the persecutions are over.

As for the conversion of Russia, it is not as clear-cut. But something has begun. The conversion movement began in the sixties soon after Khruschev, as we have said, and is actually increasing in considerable proportions with the rebirth of churches in Ukraine, Byelorussia and elsewhere.

Apparitions in the East: Medjugorje

At this point we must cite an intermediary phenomenon: Medjugorje's apparitions in Yugoslavia, which today have an influence throughout the entire world and a substantial one in America.

These apparitions, which began June 24, 1981, have surfaced suddenly in an Eastern country, and it was the first time that apparitions were not crushed. Most certainly the Marxist system acted ruthlessly; it threw the priest in prison as well as many parishioners and others. I, who was investigating this apparition, suffered, after being trampled in France, tried and convicted, fined and served with a banning order.

But the message is a message of peace. Those who had to suffer because of these apparitions did so in silence; and the Communist authorities, reassured, declared in 1986 (thus well before their fall): "The phenomenon of Medjugorje is purely religious, not political, thus legal."

Most certainly, the profit from the pilgrims ant tourists was a powerful motivation. This Blessed Virgin who attracted so many dollars was worthy of consideration. But the Marxist government would have not given in for this sole reason. It had battled with Medjugorje because it saw in it the Trojan Horse of Croatian nationalism, even a return of the Oustachis. The apolitical attitude of the pilgrims, the discipline and the courtesy of all of the faithful who were, enlightened by the message, created a climate of reconciliation.

Medjugorje seemed, from this point of view, like a premonitory sign of the liberations in Yugoslavia. And this phenomenon has radiated to the eastern countries from which people came on pilgrimage.

In October, 1981, long before perestroika, Medjugorje's prophets revealed this double message I reproduced in my book, Did the Blessed Virgin appear to Medjugorje? published at the beginning of 1984:

In Poland,a short time from now, great conflicts will come but the righteous will win. The great conflicts did suddenly appear on the following December 13, but ended well, as we have seen.

The message of the same day added, in the way of Fatima: Russia is the people in which God will be the most glorified.

It would take too long to place in this saga the apparitions in the Ukraine from which I just returned.

Conclusion

The convergence of these promises, facts and results can only be left to be appreciated by each one of us individually.

I will thus simply conclude in an entirely open manner this free appreciation:

1. Catholic Poland heavily contributed to the event of the century, the end of a Marxist dictatorship in the Eastern countries. It is really the case of an inner and profound Christian movement that has always avoided political involvement. It was because this movement was apolitical that it had political weight, and the most determinant part was the union and purely secular weight of the union Solidarity that Lech Walesa created under a deeply personal Christian inspiration in explicit adherence to Cardinal Wyszynski's consecration. In his most crucial union and national negotiations and in the clandestine broadcast he agreed to give last year on French television, Walesa, above the Solidarity insignia, the image of Our-Lady of Czestochowa.

The liberation theology which sought to be political did not liberate anybody. The Polish religious movement, carefully apolitical, has liberated Poland and, step by step, neighboring countries. It is the clearest part of the document.

2. The Christian resistance of the East has gradually pierced the misinformation, thanks to modest and brave Bulletins: Eastern Christians, Aid to the Faithful of the USSR, Istina, etc. The survival of Christianity and the rebirth of conversions in youth have refuted the Marxist science that was announcing the spontaneous disappearance of religions. This disappearance did not happen. And the most terrible persecution of all time, the longest, along with psychiatric hospitals, Siberia and everything else, did not get anywhere. This blow was fatal to Marxism and to the Marxists themselves. The prestige acquired by those who were not afraid and did resist by keeping faith played a considerable role in the new stage.

3. Fatima and Medjugorje's prophecies about the end of persecutions in Russia and the conversion of its people had seemed unlikely for a long time. Today they become likely. Persecution has ended. The phenomenon of conversions has started; how far will it go? I am not qualified to answer this question.

It only seems that Christianity, modest and often depreciated during these last few years, plays an unknown role in the world, a role that is more important that it seems. It is a moral force, a calm, by no means fanatic, energy that maintains a respect for God and the defense of man. It is an essentially nonviolent, peaceful role.

It was the mistake of many Christians in the Occident to unite the class struggle as a necessary means to social or political progress, and to flatter the torturous regime.

Medjugorje's message is the opposite of these combative methods. In the country where all these factions were (these Balkans where the adjective "Balkanize" comes from), the visceral tensions were serious and numerous, inextricable at all levels- tensions between Christians and Moslems, be-

23

tween Catholic Croatians and Orthodox Serbs, between Christians and the atheist government - Medjugorje's message took the opposite side of the traditional struggles.

Our Lady was saying to Medjugorje's Croatians: "Love your Moslem Croatian brothers, love your Orthodox Serb brothers, love those who govern you." This is what allowed for so many reconciliations. Only love wins the true victories.

The Figaro asked Father Rene Laurentin for a Great Conference on the Churches as the driving force behind liberations in the East, Because of his numerous trips to these countries during the terrible years.

To bring up to date, at the last hour, he traveled to these countries: Poland (September), Yugoslavia (October), Romania and the USSR (November and beginning of December, 1990). His interviews are arranged according to the principal points of interest: Russia (Moscow), the Ukraine, including the apparitions in Grouchevo, Romania and Poland with an evocation of the prayer to martyred Poland, the secret source of its victory.

The preceding text represents an analysis and a synthesis of the Christian lines of power that have promoted liberation in the East. This text had been written before the November-December trip. The conference which was freely made on December 14 showed a few illustrative flashes.

These lines of power were and are today, men and women - human beings. Many have died, ignored, resisting until the end in the desolation of their prison cells, in hard labor camps, with temperatures below 50 celsius, in Siberia, or in psychiatric hospitals. Some have survived. They had to be met. A few of them had to be known, in their diversity, because they represent the hidden face of this immense current of deep freedom that continues to dramatically progress, in spite of so many antagonistic forces.

Today's Catholics have become masochists. They hide their saints and their martyrs, or even sulk, minimize or criticize them. This truth, is shameful.. Christians from the West have the privilege to exercise their faith in easy and comfortable conditions. They often take advantage of it becoming inert and cowardly. The Christians from the East are a big lesson. Here is what they have made of their faith. Secrets, lies and betrayals were hiding their solitary heroism. It is great news that we can finally know about it. These are only a few significant cases inside an enormous mass that could fill libraries. The full story is written in Heaven only, in God's heart and light.

Book II

RUSSIA

1

Visit to the priests of the Supreme Soviet,
artisans of the law on religious freedom:

Gleb Yakounine, during his interview, in his
office at the Supreme Soviet in Moscow.

GLEB YAKOUNINE

deputy today, after 5 years in prison

Monday, November 26, 1990: Here I am, overwhelmed, at
the door of the Supreme Soviet: a large, practical building;
a big cube without solemnity. I expect to be searched and

meticulously checked. No I enter here more easily than I would the Vatican today, where the assassination attempt against the Pope has complicated everything; and I move about without hindrance, through corridors and elevators, among deputies, military or civil, men or women, who wear the Soviet insignia with the hammer and sickle.

I advance towards the office of Father Yakounine. Arrested in November 1979, kept in solitary confinement for a long time, he had been freed on April 4, 1987. He is no. 1720 (17th story, no 20).

I have arrived. Gleb Yakounine is there, wearing a light blue cassock, with a chain and gold cross, naturally. He has a large forehead, hair combed back, and a red beard. His silhouette stands out against the large bay windows looking over the Loskowa and the Stalinist cathedrals. His schedule is busy; others are waiting for him. I come straight to the point:

R. LAURENTIN - Gleb Yakounine, it is said today that the government is interested in the moral values of Christianity. Why?

G. YAKOUNINE - The crisis in our country inclines us to search for new resources. On the other hand, power is moving towards democracy. It must look for a support from religion, in order to establish a new majority. Moreover, *glasnost* has introduced a profound change in mentality.

R.L. - And the law on religious freedom, where does it stand?

G.Y. - On Oct. 1st it was voted on for all of the Union (USSR); on October 25, for Russia. It is being enforced.

R.L. - You were a member of the drafting commission. Are you satisfied with the law, or is it a first step?

G.Y. - It is a fundamental law. There is only one negative aspect.It does not really defend the rights of religious groups wanting to leave the hierarchy of the Church. It is very important to our situation. During the thirties, at Stalin's instigation, the KGB had eliminated what was left of the rights of the Church, and the Catholic Church of the Ukraine was then eliminated. In 1943 the State relaxed the repression on the Orthodox Church; but it was in order to gain its support during the war, that the new legislation was then structured in such a way as to make the hierarchy of the Church an instrument of the KGB.

R.L. - Those who are not sufficiently supported - is it the new independent Ukrainian Church? Or are you thinking about Baptists and sects?

G.Y. - I speak of the religious organizations that want to leave the Orthodox hierarchy.

I did not understand the meaning of the statement at first; I realized it later. In this same office, two women, representatives of their church, also came to Yakounine to defend the case of their Church The parish priest, an Orthodox, had himself ordained bishop by another hierarchy which was cut off from the official Church. He did this in order to assure a spiritual rebirth with which his numerous faithful seemed satisfied. But the Church he acquired and remodeled was broken into and taken away from him. The Metropolite Juvenal came to take it back officially.

R.L.- Were you the only priest in this commission who drew up this law?

G.Y. - No, the president of this committee is also a priest - Father Polocin. He is in the office next to mine, No. 1719.

There have always been priests and bishops at the *Supreme Soviet*, but they were official Orthodox more or less close to the KGB. Today, there are more of them, and the dissidents of yesterday are well-placed. This would have not been unthinkable in 1988 and even in 1989.

R.L. - During the drafting of this law, did you think you were well listened to?

G.Y. - Yes.

R.L. - In previous years you were outlawed?

G.Y. - Yes, from 1979 to 1984, I was imprisoned in Moscow.

R.L. - A hard prison?

G.Y. - Yes, very hard.

R.L. - What was hard? The food, the cold, the living conditions? Like it was in Romania?

G.Y. - No, the prison in Moscow was materially well organized. It was hard, less physically than morally.

R.Y.- What do you mean?

G.Y. - Pressure from the KGB.

R.L. - Were you alone in your cell?

G.Y. - No, I was with informants, prisoners sold to the KGB; they all lectured me in the same way. I was going from judges to informers, armed with the same ideas, the same pressure. Psychologically, it was intolerable, as well as the total lack of contact with an order and the realities of the outside world. Nothing else to read but *Pravda* (the organ of the Party). I was continuously filled with the same ideas. No books, no contact with close ones and friends. Freedom was asphyxiated.

R.L. - This is interesting. It is similar to the Devil's tactic to neutralize those he fears. He imposes without respite the same obsessions: enough to drive you crazy. Is that what explains Father Doudko's public retraction, he who was a hero of the Faith?

G.Y. - It was during his second incarceration. He was first sent to Siberia, under Stalin, he was freed. He started giving his prophetic sermons. He was arrested again. He was then worn down, exhausted. He is not the only one who succumbed in such a way. Kracin, a Georgian dissident who resides in the USA, wrote a book to explain the mechanisms of this wearing down. His book is entitled *The Judgement*.

R.L. - Were you able to say Mass?

G.Y. - No, it was not allowed, and there was no means to do it.

R.L. _ Were you able to pray?

G.Y. - Of course.

R.L. - Mostly at night?

G.Y. - During the day also.

R.L. - What do you hope for the future?

G.Y. - Fatima's predictions for the end of persecutions, the conversion of Russia to start happening.

R.L.- Do you think Russia is on its way to conversion?

G.Y. - There is political change. At the moral level, it is a lot more difficult. The difficulties come from the religious administration, infiltrated by the KGB, which has recruited, set up its agents.

These people regret the past and paralyse the future. The members of the Episcopate were, for the most part, submissive to the KGB.

R.L. - Even now?

G.Y. - They talk with the KGB; they cooperate. It is always difficult to change a certain mentality. They have nostalgia for the past.

R.L. - Even among priests?

G.Y. - Yes, priests and hierarchy. In Romania, the elimination was requested. We have the same problem here. Now that the KGB is losing official control of religious organizations, there are many people who escape the influence of the KGB. It creates a better climate for faith to grow. But what is left of this dependence creates a disaffection with the official Church. In the Ukraine, for example, there is pressure to secede, and some people leave the official Church. Soon this can come to Moscow.

The two women who came to defend the case of their dissident Church are a living illustration of this point.

R.L. - Do your duties as deputy allow you to occupy a ministry on Sunday?

G.Y. - Yes, in the town of Chelkovo, 30 kilometers from Moscow, in the parish of Nikolski.

R.L. - How many baptisms are there each Sunday in this parish?

G.Y. - Between 10 and 30.

R.L. - Is it the same in all of the parishes?

G.Y. - Yes, along with many baptisms of adults.

R.L. - Difficulties?

G.Y. - The shortage of printing houses. There are only clandestine ones that produce sparingly. Petric, who supervises the printing department at the Moscow Patriarchate, does everything to slow down or sabotage these activities in spite of the enormous need to spread religious instruction. They do like the apparatchiks for *perestroika*. While this is going on, Baptists are able to distribute 250,000 Gospels (millions should be printed). The official structures are deficient. Around Moscow, groups appear which do not acknowledge the official religion, for example, this community founded by a certain Kritchkov (dissident Baptists, if I understood it well).

R.L. - What are you expecting from the Occident?

G.Y. - First of all, religious literature.

R.L. - I am going to the Ukraine: How is the situation there?

G.Y. - It is the tragedy of secession. Patriarch Alexis (Moscow) allowed an Orthodox Patriarchate to be instituted in Kiev. He granted full powers and independence to the Church of the Ukraine with an unresolved judicial situation.

He gave to the Metropolite of this Republic the title "the Blessed". This patriarchal title does not belong to a Metropolite, and this one was used as a tool of the KGB to oppress the Greek-Catholic Church.

R.L. - In the Ukraine, isn't the problem the division and the competition between the official Church on its way to independence, the independent Orthodox Church which was just established, and the Catholic Church which is coming out of the underground? Isn't the problem this rivalry between the three Ukrainian Churches?

G.Y. - Competition, emulation, are good things. They are better than stagnation.

2

Father Poloin, President of the Commission that devised the law on religious freedom

FATHER POLOCIN

President of the commission that devised the Law on religious freedom

Here I am in Father Polocin's office, which is not as busy. The President of the Commission for the Law on Religious Freedom gave it the look of a monastic cell. He is not a fighter like Yakounine is; he is a calm, solid, serene, courteous man.

All throughout our interview, he picks up the phone, which rings incessantly, and hangs it up without trying to find out who is calling. After repeating this gesture at least ten times, he just turns it off. He wears a black cassock, a black beard, a cross upon his chest, and two insignias which I will later talk about to him.

R. Laurentin - Was the Christians' role important in the recent liberation by *glasnost*?

Policin- Their role was decisive. All the history of our country was determined by the attitude of the Russians towards Christ. All the historical events, all the tragedies, all the successes come from the attitude of the Christians, like the Jews in the Bible.

R.L. - And liturgical?

P. - In a way. But this second trait was more characteristic of the Byzantium rite than Russia.

R.L. - But you have splendid services, compelling chants that talk about the people...

P. - ...even when people don't understand, which is often the case now, they are affected. Even young people go to church. But the missionary activities and the conversion of everyday life do not really happen.

R.L. - The Christians who are persecuted, in prison or in psychiatric hospitals, have they played an important role in this liberation?

P. - They have saved the Orthodox Church's honor at a time when the hierarchies were lying, glorifying Stalin, then Breshnev. They truly have saved the Church. Now is the time for consolidation and dialogue.

R.L. - After 70 years of atheism, what is being done for oral catechism and teaching?

P. - Too little is being done because the Orthodox Church has lost the tradition of catechism. Our big problem, is not enough staff to take care of it. Priests who devote themselves to it are rather rare.

R.L. - Have you had difficulties these last few years? Did you spend time in prison?

P.- No, no jail time, but I was not allowed to exercise my ministry, because then each priest had to be registered by the *Official Committee on Religious Affairs*, an organ of the government.

R.L. - Did this limit your freedom?

P. - Of course, because if we ignored it, we were persecuted. Not being registered, I could not do anything. The Church was leaving me free to exercise; the government did not allow it.

R.L.- You could not preach, or celebrate Mass?

P.- No.

R.L. - Then, what could you do? A monastic life? How did you spend your days?

I stress this fact without getting anything else than this answer:

P. - I was on unemployment. But, after two years, I was given an administrative function, part-time, in a printing house belonging to the Patriarchate. And I was paid under an assumed name. It was only at the time of millennium that I was able to become a priest again.

R.L.- Where did you exercise your ministry?

P. - A hundred kilometers from Moscow, in Obninsk.

R.L. - Did you have an official car to go there?

P. - I just bought one last week (the week of November 18, 1990), but I do not know how to drive yet.

R.L. - Then you have a driver?

P. - No, I am learning in order to get my license.

R.L. - In this parish, how many baptisms a week?

P. - This summer, from 30 to 70; now from 5 to 10 or 15.

R.L. - Does the Law on freedom satisfy you?

P. - Yes, I presided over its making.

R.L. - Did you have problems?

P. - A lot of work.

R.L. - But what about fundamental difficulties?

P. - They have been resolved.

R.L. - What are you expecting from this law in terms of the transformation of the country?

P. - This law makes all religious activities legal. It ends the registration of priests by the government. They are no longer dependent on authorizations from the State. They only have to be priests to exercise. The State does not meddle in the Church's affairs and cannot do anything against religion anymore. It only keeps its role as guardian of public order.

R.L. - Does religion have as much freedom for its propaganda as atheism does?

P. - Today religion has much more freedom than atheism, because atheism is not a program supported by the State anymore. It only has its clients, and they are not too many. Atheists can only propose conferences. With us, you do not get speeches and interminable discussion, but catechism, confession, training, liturgy.

R.L. - Yes, Christian Praxis! Do you think Fatima's prophecy is on its way?

P. - I think so, but what will be the future, I cannot say. There are new signs. The Russian people do not fight God anymore. Will the Russian people continue to change? The future will decide. The Church will now speak. It has a radical responsibility.

R.L.- The two insignias you wear on your cassock, what is their meaning? Here, on the right side, the colored insignia of the deputies, and above, a silver insignia on which I see the Greek sign of Christ?

P. - The first insignia means that I am a deputy. The other one was given to me by the delegation of the Orthodox Church in Jerusalem. This one I wear underneath to emphasize the Christian priority.

R.L. - Your colleague Yakounine does not wear the deputy insignia. Isn't he also a deputy?

P. - Yes, of course, but without wearing the insignia.

R.L. - Why?

P. - He does not want to wear the Party's insignia; the hammer and sickle. Myself, I have found another solution by putting this image underneath the other one.

R.L. - How do you explain that Father Doudko, who was a first-rate believer and prophet, retracted publicly on television a few years ago?

P. - I do not know what means the KGB employed, but he was conditioned and forced.

R.L. - He is in France now, where he testifies about his faith and this accident. And what about the recent murder of Father Men? Is there an investigation? What's its status?

P. - The investigation is in progress, but it is not being rushed. This means that political forces were involved in this affair.

R.L. - What do you hope for the future of the Church in Russia?

P. - That God does not say again to our Church what he said to the Angel of Laodicea or other Churches in the *Apocalypse*[1].

R.L. - Are you expecting anything from the West?

P.- I wish for communication between priests from the West, Catholics, Protestants. What matters to us is to find the Orthodox tradition again, its cosmic and Christian dimension, so that people of all ages and beliefs understand how God works in the world. It is important to detect the signs of relations between God and Man. But right now, most people do not see that. They stay on the outside.

R.L. - The outside of what?

P. - Ceremonies. But what is missing is religious instruction, inner rediscovery, training. We would like to share in the experiences of the West.

R.L. - For monastical life?

P. - In that, we have our experience. The problem for us is mostly to rebuild the disorganized parishes. The Vatican II's perspectives are of great interest to us.

"The victim and the executioner" Ogorodnikov on his way out of his office at the Party, localized in the city hall dedicated to Dzerjinsky, the founding fatheic Party in the USSR

ALEXANDER OGORODNIKOV

9 years spent prison

Here I am before Alexander Ogorognidkov (40 years old on last March 27) in the office of the Christian Democratic Party he created. Paradoxically this Party is located in the City Hall of the district of Dzerjinski, the famous founder of the Tcheka, which became the KGB. Alexander, schooled in atheism, full of energy, had belonged to the Komosol (the Communist Youth). He was expelled in 1971, as well as from the Cinema Institute, and was baptized in 1973. He started the Obchina Community. In 1974 the KGB offered him emigration. He refused: " It is you who should emigrate!" He was arrested and imprisoned successively in five camps, until his unexpected liberation in 1987, on the demand of Sakharov and Margaret Thatcher. He founded the Christian Communities Bulletin in four languages (Russian, English, German, Italian). He fights for the defense of rights and freedoms; he gives life to the political party he created while giving food and clothing to the poor whose number is growing in Moscow. The interview is delayed. The telephone headquarters tells him his phone number is going to be changed... so that his relations with foreign countries will be cut off. He protests with calm and persuasion. A detail catches my attention, his long hair tied in a tuft, combed back, similar to the hairstyle of certain popes.

Rene Laurentin - You are not a priest?

Ogorodnikov - No.

R.L. - Does your long hair have religious meaning?

O. - It is an Orthodox tradition, even among lay people, and it was a way to differentiate myself from people belonging to the regime.

R.L. - How did you go from atheism to baptism?

O.- It was in 1973. I was a college student. Since childhood I had been educated in hardcore atheism. Lenin's portrait was hanging above my bed.

R.L. - And you were a Communist militant?

45

O. - Yes, unfortunately! I was fighting faith (how awful) at the level of arguments. I thought the Church would disappear by itself.

R.L. - But where did your change of mind come from?

O. - From contact with reality.

R.L. - And with God?

O. - It was a long, hard journey.

He has a hard time expressing himself. Is the subject too personal or is it fatigue and illness?

R.L. - Be more precise.

O. - (He sighs.) Marxism had disappointed me and I was looking for truth beyond the realm of ideologies, those from here and from the West.

R.L. - But what about God?

O. - Dostoyevsky showed me the truth.

R.L. - But how?

O. - It is a rather logical progression. At that time, I was looking for God through reason, abstractly. It was the beginning of my journey.

His confidences are definitely hindered by his modesty.

R.l. - And now?

O. - I have arrived to living experience. Pasoloni's film ("*The Gospel According to Matthew*") played an important role in this.

R.L. - With your functions as head of a party, do you find time to pray?

O. - Yes, because without prayer, I lose strength and hope.

One can see, because of a certain feebleness, that he carries in him the after-effects of his long period of captivity. His supple and rare energy is the fruit of a struggle.

R.L. - Faith caused you to go to prison. Where?

O. - In Ural.

R.L. - Which camp?

O.- Several camps. I was often transferred in order to cut off my contacts with the other prisoners who listened to me.

R.L. - How many camps?

O. - Five.

R.L. - The hardest one?

O. - Perm 36.

It is the name of the camp, not of the town.

R.L. - What did you suffer from: cold - hunger?

O. - Yes, a lot. The three constant torments were cold, hunger, and this duration without end.

R.L. - How did you manage not to go crazy?

O. - Through prayer, particularly the *Prayer to Jesus*. I also tried to write a script for a film - in my memory, because we did not have paper - a movie about the spiritual renewal in Russia.

R.L. - Do you hope to make this film?

O. - Yes, because we have founded a cinema center in our party.

He does not give any more details on the camps and the pain Nikita Struve wrote about in Paris.

R.L. - Were you also interrogated?

O. - Yes, but I did not answer.

R.L.- Were you tortured?

O.- Beaten several times. The American cuffs have deformed my hands and made me lose sensation. All this violence because I was refusing to give up my cross.

R.L. - Did they end up taking it by force?

O. - I had put it in my mouth. They tried to make me give it up by using tear gas. They also tried to pull it out. While this fight was going on, I was praying. One of the officers reacted. "It's me you should beg!'

R.l. - Were they also informers in your prison?

O. - Yes, when I was not in solitary confinement.

R.L. - These KGB agents, were they prisoners or policemen?

O. - Both.

R.L. - What did they talk about?

O. - Their propaganda: "Redeem yourself and you will be set free," etc.

R.L. - How do you feel now in this most official city hall?

O. - It may not be quite legal. Our party deputy, who belonged to this district, gave up their office to us. In principle, it is the office of the *Soviet Commission of the District*.

R.L. - How many deputies do you have?

O. - Two at City Hall and they are sympathizers, three at the *Supreme Soviet*, and one at the Russian Parliament. He does not belong to our party, but he expresses our point of view.

R.L. - Are you happy with the current developments?

O. - Not happy at all. We feel the reaction. We are moving towards a harsher regime.

R.L. - Gorbachev's *glasnost* still helped some?

O. - *Glasnost*, yes, but it is the people's *glasnost*, not Gorbachev's. He created it as a means to save the corpse of Communism.

R.L. - What do you hope for?

O. - No other alternative than to secure the rebirth of Christianity at the spiritual and moral level in order to elevate Man, to make him responsible for his actions.

R.L. - Why did Yakounine and you, who are very close to one another, found two separate parties?

O. - You should ask Father Yakounine. I had created a party. He created another a year later, when he saw our success. This duality is detrimental to our movement.

R.L. - But what _does_ differentiate your two parties?

O. - It's hard to say. They probably are more conservative than we are, but I don't have enough specific knowledge about his program. His party is uninational, orthodox, with a tendency toward monarchy. Our party is democratic and Christian; it belongs to the European family tradition. Since September, 1989, there has been an international federation of Christian democracies. We belong to it. Our values are love, freedom and solidarity.

R.L. - This brings you closer to Walesa. Are you happy about his election?

O. - Of course.

R.L. - Yakounine criticizes the Orthodox hierarchy. What about you?

O. - Hierarchy is a disease of the Church. We are as strict as Yakounine is. But we know that this is also our disease because together we form the Body of Christ. By criticizing our hierarchy, we criticize ourselves.

R.L. - Do you see the Christian role as important to the liberation movement that has progressed this year?

O. - Yes, it is important. But it started a long time ago, as early as 1977 Christians started a human rights movement.

R.L. - Yes, but Sakharov played a considerable role in this area. And he was an agnostic.

O. - The Christian movement was more numerous and stronger.

R.L. - What was its mode of action?

O. - Not solely the defense of human rights. Above all, the fight for the rebirth of Christian values, for the freedom of the Church. And we try to make the most of Christian ideas.

R.L. - Do you know Josyp Teryela, the Ukrainian? What do you think of him?

O. - He is fantastic.

R.L. - But now he has been deported to Toronto.

O. - Deported, I don't think so.

R.L. - That's what he told me.

O. - I know what's what. They also tried to make me agree to emigrate, by using seductive incentives. I didn't agree. I don't think he would have left if he had not wanted to.

R.L. - Maybe he wanted to end the pain his successive captivities had inflicted upon his fiancee and family. What do you think of the apparitions in the Ukraine; notably Grouchevo?

O. - Authentic!

R.L. - Do you know of others in the Ukraine?

O. - Yes, Pochevo, near an Orthodox monastery.

R.L. - Are they still happening?

O. - I don't know.

R.L. - How do you explain that a Christian such as Doudko retracted his position?

O. - I think he gave in because he relied too heavily on his own strength.

R.L. - Did he regain the integrity his Christian inner light had brought him?

O. - Yes, his actions are excellent.

R.L. - How do you see the future?

O. - I am counting on God. I am sure the Lord will not abandon Russia, nor world Christianity.

R.L. - Do you have any project?

O. - The Party I founded, the journal I gave you, a project for a movie, a school for Christian training, and then the program for the spiritual rebuilding of our party: Freedom, Responsibility, Solidarity. Renew Man in God's image. We are against liberal ideologies.

R.L. - Are you still a Socialist?

O. - No.

R.L. - Capitalist?

O. - Neither.

R.L. - Is there a *tertium quid*?

O. - Yes, a program for social freedom, with a free market economy, free enterprise, and responsibility toward one's fellow human, notably the disenfranchished, the underprivileged. Finally *sobornost.*

This untranslatable Russian word, elaborated upon by Russian theologians (Boulgakov, Soloviev), means community, in the theological and mystical fullness of the meaning.

Ogorodnikov takes interest in those who suffer from the ever more tragic scarcity in Moscow. On the morning of the day I met him, it had just been announced that there was no more milk, and there would be no more. Ogorodnikov, who receives many donations from his interviews in Western journals, has obtained a room in the basement of the City Hall. He takes me to see it. There are tons of packages from Holland (legumes, pasta, etc.) and tons of clothes. It will really be needed in the tragic situation that could bring on a revolt, which would be followed by the radical takeover that nostalgic people of the old regime wish for.

Coming back from the basement, we walk in front of the bust of the father of the KGB, Dzejinski. I ask Ogorodnikov to pose in front of the bust.

O. - No! He motioned with a meaningful gesture.

R.L. - Too bad, it was to immortalize the executioner and the victim!

He smiles.

O. - Then it's okay!

The photograph is taken. Ogorodnikov is a determined man, ardent, luminous; he has suffered enormously from starting programs that go beyond human capacities, and his own capacities have been weakened by nine years in prison. But he is always calm, attentive, active, shining from a smile that comes from the depths within. When he returned from his nine years in captivity, his wife had disappeared. The woman he married next did not tolerate the invasion of his house by all the people who turn to Ogorodnikov. She left. How does he live this serenely with so many ordeals, a task so enormous? He had hesitated, out of modesty, to answer my previous questions about prayer. He answered when we talked about his captivity. Prayer is his secret to keep strength and hope. How long will he last under these conditions, with this wear and tear one can only imagine, despite his youth and dynamism? He belongs to this world without being in this world. It would not be surprising to see him fly away like Elijah on a chariot of fire.

3

TATIANA GORITCHEVA

Founder of The Russian Feminist Movement *Mary*

Tatiana Goritcheva is one of those top intellectuals, brought up in atheism, who were converted in the 70's. Deported in 1980, she was able to come back to her country in 1988, and today testifies freely (including on television)about her spiritual discoveries. I questioned her during a visit to France in September 1990.

R. Laurentin - Tatiana Goritcheva, you are considered a convert from atheism.

Tatiana Goritcheva - We are all converts. The nation is converted. Our Church is filled with neophytes. I am a witness of this conversion.

R.L. - But you, how did you get there?

T.G.- I was brought up in atheism. I was a militant Communist. I took Philosophy at the University of Leningrad. But I had read Nietzsche and Heidegger. I taught Philosophy. I was a psychoanalyst. I did it all. But something was missing and I looked for salvation in yoga. It was forbidden. We were learning to meditate with mantras, formulas we repeated. I don't know how I found the *Pater*. I started to recite it. And the obvious revealed itself - *it was true*. From then on, liturgy and starets (spiritual masters) replaced yoga, which I then quit. Conversions are unexpected things. They occur like a miracle... very naturally. Now, to me, being at Church is like being at home, free of all my problems, all my anxieties.

R.L. - You founded a feminist movement under the patronage of the Blessed Virgin. Its name *Mary*. This would be surprising in America where the feminist movements attack the Blessed Virgin as a dangerous myth.

T.G. - The Blessed Virgin is part of our roots. The Mother of God reaches us at the deepest level. I have not found a country where the Mother of God is as loved. At home, there is no need for charities, movements. We rely on the Mother of God, on the Liturgy. There are many icons. Maria is the icon of all that was lost. We were lost in atheism. The Church was destroyed. The monasteries were closed down. To speak of God was to go to prison. But it is said that the Mother of God comes to Hell... at its deepest level, to save the greatest sinners, to the last circle of the abyss. That is what she has done for me and for many in Russia.

R.L. - A feminist movement is a liberation movement, usually against domination by males. What is your position on that?

T.G. - Our movement was more radical. It attack Marxist atheism, which destroys the masculinity of men and the femininity of women. Women are the ones who carry the burden because of the immaturity and alcoholism of men.

R.L. - When did you found this *Mary* movement?

T.G. - In 1979.

R.L. - How did you choose that name?

T.G. - We definitely were looking for a name. And without consulting one another, everybody said, right away, *Mary*, the Mother of God.

R.L. - Did you have problems?

T.G. - Our journal was seized. We were beat up. I was beat up. It was forbidden to talk about the Mother of God. Finally we were deported.

R.L. - Yes, a feminist movement was scandalous for Communists which proclaimed it had resolved the feminine problem... by promoting women to hard manual labor and driving big tractors rather than to the *Supreme Soviet*. But what changed in your life, after this conversion?

T.G. - We visited prisons, psychiatric hospitals, but we were often arrested before we arrived. The women were more courageous than the men and they too were arrested. We organized conferences. People came to see us, from everywhere. But it could not go on. Everything we said was forbidden. We should have said that Trotski and Stalin were great friends of women. It was absurd. Our only weapons were love and humility. That is what the Mother of God taught us. I found humility through Grace.

R.L. - What was the role of the Christians in the change we are seeing?

T.G. - Gorbachev succeeded because he had many Christians with him. It is the spiritual foundation of *glasnost*. Before, the spiritual could only survive in old women. But the Russian culture is spiritual and there never was a Marxist culture. The Christian culture prevailed.

R.L. - I heard that Gorbachev's mother is Christian.

T.G. - I don't know her, but some of my friends do. She goes to church everyday.

R.L. - Honestly, how do you see the Church in the West?

T.G. - In your home, in the West, notably in Germany, bishops and priests are criticized. Not in our home. The Church exists, in spite of our sins, in spite of our weakness. Like Solzhenitsyn, I am sometimes surprised and disappointed by the West.

R.L. - How do you see the future of Russia and Christianity in Russia?

T.G. - We are now living in a very different situation. The Church is not persecuted anymore. Everybody is free. It is a great rebirth of faith, and everybody is for it. Even atheists are interested in the Church today. They go to church. But sometimes the Devil is faster than God. Pornography, rock and roll, drinking, tourism are common. We are in a singular situation because, under Breshnev or Andropov, many people still thought that Communism existed. They had a certain Marxist idealism; but now the ideologies are destroyed, and many people are disoriented.

R.L. - Is it as true in the city as it is in the country?

T.G. - It is the same everywhere, but it is more visible in the city, where there are churches. In the country, often, there is nothing - no church, no theater, no library, no intellectual circle - only vodka to drink. That's all.

R.L. - Vodka is still a plague?

T.G. - Very much so.

R.L. - How will this temptation be overcome?

T.G. - Today, the situation is dramatic. There is scarcity, shortage everywhere. You have to be in line even to buy apples in Moscow. There will be great hunger in Russia.

R.L. - Even with your harvests?

T.G. - Harvests? They are in total disarray.

R.L. - I heard that officials in charge of the distribution of food supply engage in the black market. They try to perpetuate the ancien regime: starvation would be the way to cause a revolt that would allow a radical takeover.

T.G. - There is a problem with that. Because of it, the Church will have a great role.

R.L. - In what way?

T.G. - Because only within the Church can you find serious men.

R.L. - The Church would feed the people?

T.G. - It can happen. The Church will do like it does in the Third World, and it's already started. People go to Church for the spiritual, but also for the material: to eat, to get money. It's started.

R.L. - What accounts for the fact that after 70 years of atheism, God has maintained such prestige?

T.G. - You see, in Russia, Communism was a religion; but man was not destroyed. Conscience was destroyed. But the Russian people have kept faith and hope. Something of God stayed at the bottom of one's heart. Even people like my father, who does not believe in it and never thought about it, is deeply Christian.

R.L. - Does he go to mass now?

T.G. - No, he does not go. He does not need to go, because he lives the spiritual deeply, with love, with sacrifice. Those are things he preserved.

R.L. - Do you think one day he will join the Church?

T.G. - Maybe. He is searching. He will find a language.

R.L. - You found God again through yoga. Did you keep or did you eliminate that technique?

T.G. - When I became Christian, I became a new creature. One cannot mix yoga and Christianity.

R.L. - Many Christians mix them, even in monasteries. What do you think of that?

T.G. - It's a little bit like black magic.

T.G. - Before I became Christian, it was possible, when I did not know who Christ was. But after, it would have been a big lie.

R.L. - What do you say to friends who try to reach Christianity through yoga?

T.G. - I do not say anything, because 90% of the time, yoga leads atheists toward the Church but one cannot stay with yoga. One must find his own roots again. It's natural.

T.L. - When Russia was open again to you, toward the end of the eighties, did you see your old friends from Mary again?

T.L. - I saw a few of them, like Gregory who founded a movement for large families, and many others.

R.L. - Are you thinking about creating another feminist movement based on the Blessed Virgin?

T.G. - I don't know... if it is God's will. Now there are many Christian movements in the Soviet Union. They are all dedicated to the Blessed Virgin, because, at home, there are no Christians who don't believe in the Blessed Virgin. The whole Church is attached to her. Russian women are always thinking about the Mother of

4

*The first expressions of
the Russian feminist movement:* Mary

In addition to the interview with Tatiana Goritcheva (1990), here are the first expressions of her movement, *Mary*. They were published in *samisdat*, in an Almanac, *Women for Women*. The first issue was published in 10 typed copies, on December 10, 1979. It was then copied in an assembly line and was very successful. A second issue was published, and the authors were expatriated from the USSR on Sunday July 20, 1980. The expression of a feminist movement in Russia would have been too much of a contradiction to the doctrine according to which this problem had been resolved by Marxism. The fact that this movement was religious and dedicated to Mary made its case worse.

In the first Almanac, Tatiana Goritcheva, who was coming back from a failure of her a first marriage, celebrates Mary in her virginity, like the other pole of the alternative in which she was fighting. She starts her article as if she were writing a letter to another woman:

> *My beloved sister,*
>
> *On this day of the Assumption of the Mother of God, I would like to tell you everything She represents to me [...] and how, thanks to Her, I was able to find myself again, b finding God again [...]. She lifts the malediction all the previous religions have put on the feminine. Astarte was against Jehovah. The great mother of the pagan religions embodied the irrational, the dark forces, and the body. It was only in Christianity that the complete deification of*

the body occurred [Incarnation]. Only Christian-
ity destroys the dualism between body and soul. In
Christianity, God came in the flesh [...]. The recip-
rocal dependency of the flesh and the soul reaches
a superior stage. [...]. That is why this religion does
not only overlook latent sins; hidden desires are
just as material and real: "He who looks at a
woman lustfully has already committed adultery in
his heart".

The Blessed Virgin, in her purity, is elevated
above angeles. She is unique purity. She is the
Church of Christ. She is the beautiful one. Since
childhood, the Mother of God hasn't known vulgar
or lustful desires. Nothing impure could touch her.
With the Blessed Virgin, for the first time in the
history of humanity, the perfect purification of the
flesh and the unconscious occurred. Feminity, low-
ered to the rank of the demoniac by pagan religion,
is here sanctified to such a degree, raised to a
height so inaccessible, that she becomes the vessel
that receives the Holy Spirit: "And your bowels are
more vast than the heavens!" Rejoice, O! Gold-
bearing temple of the Holy Spirit! All these things
were revealed to me during my spiritual healing
and my return to the heart of the Church. Saint
Augustine said, "Christ is the remedy to all pain. It
is the same for the Queen of the Heavens - to be
ideal, ideal woman" (p. 27-28)[2].

Mary allows us to go beyond the two archetypes of the
feminine conscience according to C.G. Jung, "Identification
with the Mother or revolt against the MOTHER". T.G.
recognized herself as the second type, which would incite
women to become "criminals, anarchists, prostitutes, aiming
for an abstract, unilateral and pseudo-masculine ideal". Thus
were the models with which girls wished to identify at school:

*"Maybe you will ask me why I talk about femi-
nine scorn,when the female is completely emancipated in our country.The female is not emancipated; it was the male made feminine. In a society
like ours, the male cannot beindependent; he cannot answer for his actions, neither canhe freely and
consciously build his life. And within thefamily
(consumed by general alcoholism), as in
theindustrial world, the female constitutes the
foundationalforce [...]. Monstrously overworked,
she is the martyr ofour time."*

Tatiana then tells me about her adventure: looking for love
through a "rushed marriage", "deception, breakup", then
"debauchery, everyday hysteria", in a desperate "everything
is allowed" (p. 32). "In our immoral paganism, we have lived
this negation of femininity that is the mark of all pagan
religion of the past."

The solution was Mary:

*"She came to us as the One who comes to save
the dying. Rejoice, Gate to Salvation! The prayer to
the Holy Mother of God helped me to discover and
to renew in myself the feminine principle in all its
purity and absoluteness. What came first was the
spiritual meaning of the principal virtue: chastity.
Before I talked about it ironically, like an obsolete
thing . The Mother of God was chaste; the monks
after her o bserved chastity as did those who live in
a Christian marriage . As well as the new Adam
atoned for the old one's sins, as well as the new Eve
freed the old Eve from the curse that weighed upon
her, she became the first representation of the
Church. The Mother of God gives feminity, and
human beings in general, its only reason for being.
She gives us the image of the perfect being"* (p.33).

Her plenitude is not suspected of a tendency

>*"asocial, static, dead, because the Mother of God is completely turned toward the outside. She listens [...]. Offered to God's will, whose word she "lays in her heart". In Her, the perfect totality of life and the sacrificed abandon to God are reunited at the same time. This is why She is called the first image of the Church. The prayer addressed to her illuminates all the depths of the unconscious [...], the depth that pushes on as far as the peaks. It rejoices in depths inaccessible to human thought."*

This letter seeks only to be a "first beginning", while anticipating the development of another theme, "the eschatological renewal tied to the coming of the Blessed Virgin to our world, pillar of virginity, Church."

In a second almanac, Svetlana SANOVA[3] addresses a response to Tatiana on the following theme:

>*"My dear sister in God! Your letter which told me how your life was sanctified by prayers to our Queen, the very Holy Virgin Mary, deeply stirred my soul, touched me by so much likeness and gave me the desire to share the fruits of my own experience with prayer."*

She tells of her life as a single mother and concludes:

>*"You described the Mother of the Heavens as an eternal chaste and pure Virgin, teacher of monks and nuns. She appears to me under a different guise, in my life as a mother - the Mother of God [...]. Through her accomplishment, by becoming the Mother of God, Mary sanctified maternity. I have neither the strength nor the right to question*

the dogma of the Immaculate Conception which has been attacked by sectarians and rationalists of all sides. We ourselves, the Russian Orthodox, as well as Catholics, accept her, and we surrender as if before a secret that cannot be grasped by the intellect. The Orthodox Russian icon gives the best basis for pious meditations on the Mother of God and maternity." (p. 102 -103).

She concludes by explaining

"how a soul that remains Christian, by dint of praying to the Mother of God, arrives at the idea and the duty of maternity. Any education from which religion is absent creates a non-chaste being, with and incoherent and disparate conscience, prone to fornication. I have also known this, romantic love or agonies of love. I have known countless torments and many failures. We decided, a friend and I, to end this state of affairs and to give birth to our first children. My friend was the first unmarried mother in her class and I, the second [...]. Unmarried mothers are now numerous and Social Security services called them single mothers."

She explains this choice as a rejection of abortion and the desire to become a mother, in a society in which "the meeting of men capable of becoming husbands and fathers" is "a problem"; she respects the other solution, "the solution of virginity and chastity" (p.106).

This Christian wave, born in USSR Marxism, is probably only one of the aspects of the Russian feminist movement. It discovered Mary in the ascent from a certain hell.

5

Between two economic systems
The surprises of free trade

The Eastern bloc countries are going through liberation and deep change. What change? For better or worse? The question is not superfluous. It has pursued me in my everyday life in the USSR, at the end of November, beginning of December. What happens to the money and supply is revealing.

I had the best and worse surprise with money in the USSR. The first one is that rubles (officially exchanged at 1 ruble for 1 franc and 5 rubles for 1 dollar) were not accepted except where you had to wait in line for several hours without being certain that anything would be left.

At the international hotel *Cosmos*, a huge fifteen-story building with more than 1,000 rooms, where there are no lines, I asked for a bottle of mineral water. It cost 1 dollar.

"But what is it in rubles?"

"No, we do not accept rubles."

I learned that in the same hotel there was another counter where the same bottles were sold in rubles. Their cost was 55 kopeks, 1/2 a ruble, almost 10 times cheaper. I discovered the disconcerting scale of prices.

I go went with my experiences by trying to eat at one of the four restaurants in the hotel. I did not like one because of its rock 'n' roll music (imported from the West) that deafened me. I tried another one. But I should have made reservations the night before. At a third it was already late. I tried to sway them. I asked them for quick service and light food, soup and salad were enough for me. How much?

"10 dollars."

After all, that is not so bad, 45 francs!

"Do you accept *travelers checks*?"

"No."

But my French banker had assured me that it was easier and safer than dollars.

"So how much in rubles?"

My insistence caused perplexity. And after interminable discussions with waiters or waitresses, they accepted me. Russians are courteous and calm.

I waited for an hour. Then came my soup, a salad (Russian), some kind of a fish mousse that was very acceptable. I thought that I was finished. But there came meat and vegetables - and ice-cream, not to mention mineral water. I asked for the check. The total was 5. 5 what? No mistake, it really was in rubles. These rubles that are officially worth a franc! I had eaten so much for 5 francs.

I thought it was an act of kindness, a gift.

"No, there are no gifts here, a Russian friend assured me."

And it was confirmed. The meals I had in diverse hotels in Russia and the Ukraine were always below 10 rubles (10 francs). It is part of the advantage the *Intourist* assures foreign visitors in these hotels where a Russian cannot enter without a permit and without difficulty. In this respect, Americans (or French) are privileged in this country, like colonists were in colonies of olden times. I was embarrassed for my humiliated Russian friends. They could not come to meet me but called me to arrange a time to meet them on the sidewalk in front of the hotel. They were prohibited from entering certain places in this paradise of dollars, in their own country.

However, I was able to ask a friend to have lunch in the hotel, staying with him in order to assure that his permit would be issued and then only when he presented his passport. But at the hotel restaurant, where rubles were accepted, he was asked to pay one and a half dollars to enter, to be paid in dollars only. Luckily I had two 1 dollar bills with me. They did not have any change. I left them to flounder, not for the money, but for my curiosity as a psycho-economical investigator. The maitre d' went to the exchange office (10 minutes). He came back empty-handed. I expressed my surprise courteously:

"But why is it *me* who must pay this half a dollar?"

"Because you are the buyer!"

I stop my investigation right there, but fifteen minutes later he came back with a 1 mark coin.

"It's more than half a dollar," he said with the pride of a benefactor.

I thanked him, knowing very well that these coins were not accepted at the exchange office.

How do you live on a salary of 200 Francs?

What I cannot understand are Russian salaries. The "normal" salary is 200 rubles in town, 160 in the country, Five

69

hundred to 1000 francs (rubles) is a very high salary. How can one live on this amount, even when prices are low?

"It's because water is free and heating hardly costs anything, a ruble a month. A subway ticket costs 5 kopecks (5 cents)."

"Then the essentials are taken care of by these low prices?"

"Yes and no. If meat costs 5 rubles a kilo, you rarely find it; and it is 40 rubles at the kolkozien market (the farmers' black market). A pack of cigarettes costs 1 ruble, but you will only find them at 20 on the black market. You can fill up your tank with 20 pounds for 16 rubles (if you wait in line at the right time), but if there is a shortage, you can find some at 1 ruble a liter on the black market. That amounts to the price before the gasoline shortage, twenty-five years ago. But in Moscow, that's expensive!"

Well, it was possible to live with 200 rubles under Breshnev, who assured sufficient supplies with authority. But today one cannot make ends meet in this worsening shortage. Not only must you stand in line for hours to obtain the essential food at normal prices, but often there is nothing left total. A third of the shops seem to be closed. What is left is to look (discreetly) for a kolkozien market, if you know where to find one. If you have a super-salary, the dollar is necessary for many products. And the value of the dollar on the black market (which I don't know) is obviously much greater than 5 rubles (probably about twenty).

Friends found me taxis I could pay for in rubles, at a good price for me, but superior to the norm: 40 rubles for a morning to pick me up at the airport and a long wait; 30 rubles for an afternoon of visits to several places far from the large city of Kiev (4 million people). But most often, I could get a taxi only if I paid in dollars (14 dollars an hour, whether driving or waiting) or at prices discussed according to an arbitrary rule that escapes my understanding, 20 times more in dollars than in rubles. It usually is the only way.

A friend, who came to pick me up in his car at the hotel for a series of interviews, found that the pumps were empty at 6:45 a.m., the right time for a slight line before opening time. But, a little bit after 7 o'clock, he found out that delivery would be 10 hours late. We went back at that fateful hour. But delivery was still uncertain, and the line was already long. My appointment at the *Supreme Soviet* could not wait. We had to go to "the black". The site was picturesque - a dump right in the heart of Moscow, with fascinating flocks of crows, hundreds of them, and behind, a 500 meter-high television tower, as I was told, but whose top has always remained hidden in the clouds. My friend warned me, "Do not take a photograph. People will believe we belong to the police and I will not get any gas." The black market is everywhere but remains forbidden and confidential.

Morality is not questioned. The regime is not questioned. There is freedom of speech without any change in structures, *glasnost* without *perestroika*. The Russian people live in an awkward position between two systems and two economies. The old one does not work anymore. The new one extends like a scholar graduated between the illicit and the tolerated. No one makes any secret of refusing rubles and demanding dollars from a foreigner.

This situation is not heartening, because nothing has been proposed to institute a new economy and new structures. The West brings a system without the instruction. Soviets admire our system of plentiful supply, like a primitive people would admire an organ concert in a cathedral. But to have the same concert in another country, we would have to train organ makers and organists, fruits of a millennial tradition. A free market economy is no less exigent.

Another aspect of the problem is equally important. There was a kind of morality in Socialism, a morality without God. But the leaders availed themselves of an ideal of liberation (against religious oppression), justice and gratuity beyond King-Money. The fact that water was free, like in the country, was a symbol (and besides it was a waste). Life had a price other than a monetary one, and it was different.

This morality was not working very well, it will be said. Because it lacked God, it was missing its foundation. It did not prevent sadness, depression, boredom, and alcoholism. But (with the aid of human nature and underground religion), this morality endured a regulation - as long as the propaganda of the Communist leaders and the teaching of dialectical materialism, relayed by the organization of the *Communist Youth*, worked. But, by the beginning of the seventies, they were not working anymore. Ogorodnikov, a generous man, was enlisted in the *Communist Youth* in high school. He had been cheered for this way of freedom, for the fight against illusion and repression of religions - enemies and opiate of the people. But his personal morality was ahead of the Marxist "morality". This mystic was trouble, already disenfranchised. He was expelled from the *Communist Youth* at age 21 (1971), and was baptized in 1972. He was one case among others, with Tatiana Goritcheva and her feminist friends in 1980.

God's secret

Our triumphant capitalism does not solve the problems of the Eastern countries. It finds more profitable opportunities than it brings immediate solutions. If it brings generous gifts, it also disseminates the taste for profit, the reign of money, rock music, prostitution and drugs, not to mention unemployment. This makes the state of malaise worse than before, according to the expression from the Gospels.

Gorbachev, who was unpopular in the USSR because his *perestroika* (rebuilding) does not work, has understood the importance of finding moral values again. That is the reason he looks for the support of the Church and several priests have a seat on the *Supreme Soviet*. On this point, is his contribution understood?

The other side of the alternative for these countries would be serious. If the triumph of the West does bring on moral deterioration, it would be a catastrophe.

The economic deterioration is becoming catastrophic. During my stay in Moscow last November 27, Russian television announced to the already starving people that there would be no more milk in Moscow. The Ukraine and other producing countries were not delivering any more. This is serious. For babies, the deficiency in calcium can be disastrous. The present slump is not an empty claim for the everyday life of the Soviet citizen, even if trained to be patient.

One of the scenarios of the outcome could be the following: the increased scarcity causes one to yearn for the time under Breshnev (like the Hebrews yearned for food from their captivity in Egypt when crossing the desert). Many, including the youth, are starting to talk in such terms. This could provide support for the hard-liners of the Party, those who have not given up, and could completely maintain a system which is ready to function again. Some add that the apparachiks, responsible for distribution, stockpile produce voluntarily to cause famine and revolt, which would allow a takeover with a large support from the people. Neither is Communism out of resources. It has already proved it in Romania, Serbia and elsewhere. We must be careful not to unconsciously help them.

Our Lady of Fatima not only predicted the end of the persecutions, but the conversion of Russia, which is gaining ground through tens of thousands of baptisms every Sunday.

Some will smile on Fatima at the thought of Fatima's part in these changes, like I myself smiled at these visionary promises. But in Moscow, the priests who hold a seat on the *Supreme Soviet* talked to me spontaneously about Fatima's prophecies and did not smile.. The Orthodox deputies in Cassock, Yakounine and Polocin, believe it. Fatima has become the ecumenical element in the USSR.

Our Western materialism does not have any reason to smile. Man created by God for God needs God in this world, and in the hereafter from which He calls us.

Humor in the USSR

It is in Kiev that a young man told me this joke. On morning, Gorbachev looks out his window at the Kremlin and is surprised. Nobody is in the street! Strange! He calls his Prime Minister: "What's going on? Why is there nobody in the street?" "Yesterday you said that from now on people were allowed to live in the Soviet Union freely. Well, they all left. Myself, I was leaving when you called. Goodbye, Mister President."

This black humor is inspired by the poverty that reigns in Moscow and, less seriously, elsewhere.

Important dates

in the Ukrainian Catholic Church

1596	By the Union of Brest-Ltovsk, a part of the Ukrainian Orthodox Church is joined to Rome.
1654	Cossacks place the Ukraine under the protection of the Muscovite Tsar thwart Poland.
18th century	The Ukrainian language and literature are forbidden by Tsar Alexander II. Western Ukraine is united with the Austro-Hungarian Empire.
Jan. 22, 1919	The two parts of Ukraine (east and west) become one independent state - the National Ukrainian Republic.
1920-1922	The Soviet power recovers this nation in spite of its resistance.
1931-1933	Large-scale Stalinist persecutions - 7 million dead.
1934	Stalin annihilates the Ukrainian elite systematically 500,000 dead.
1941	The Ukraine tries to regain its independence by taking advantage of the Nazi invasion After the war, Stalin starts the persecutions again and sends 2 million Ukrainians to Siberia. He intensifies Russianization and the suppression of Ukrainian schools.
1946	Suppression of the Greek-Catholic Church. Stalin turns it over to the Orthodoxy.
1961	Levko Lukianenko is sentenced to the death penalty, reduced to detention until 1976. He leads the Ukrainian group from Helsinki.
1987	With *perestroika*, liberations have started.
Fall, 1990	After an ecumenical meeting in Moscow, the Catholic Church regains the greater majority of its churches.

Book III

UKRAINE

Ukraine, wealth of the USSR

In fact, it produces

-50% of the Soviet iron
-25% of the coal
-30% of the fruits
-25% of the vegetables, milk and meat
-25% of the cereals.

It has state-of-the-art industries for oil refining organic chemistry, aeronautics, machine tools, and precision equipment because, in spite of the destruction of the elite by Stalin, the intelligentsia and Ukrainian efficiency were reformed irresistibly. In 1989, by virtue of the structural reform on prices, Ukraine recorded an excess of 7 billion rubles from exportation (especially from sugar, oil seeds, cereals, iron minerals, steel, electronics, computers, etc.).

Russia installed 40% of its nuclear industry in the Ukraine. Placing all the risks, from which Chernobyl there. The Ukrainian Parliament decided to devote 45 to 50 billion rubles per year for the protection of the environment (instead of 10 billion in the quinquennial plan that is now ending) and demands reparations from Russia, because the consequences of Chernobyl. It remain serious to both environment and health, at long distances from the nuclear source. Ukraine is the second largest Union State in terms of population (52 million people) and surface area.

On July 16, 1990, the Ukrainian Parliament proclaimed its sovereignty by 355 ballots against 4 absentees. It is not yet a declaration of autonomy or independence, but it is very radical. It declares the primacy of Ukrainian laws over the Federation's laws, the right to raise its army and to issue its own money, which   the Baltic Republic did not do. The Parliament established a Ukrainian citizenship that protects the rights of the Russian minority (21%).

1

Msgr. Volodimir Sterniuk, Metropolite of Lvov
(Russian: Lvov) during my visit in November-
December 1990

Arrival in Lvov

First steps in the regained earthly paradise

*The Ukrainian Greek-Catholic Church had been elimi-
nated by Stalin. He had given this Church as a gift (body and
wealth) to the Orthodox Patriarchate he controlled. This
elimination was part of a plan to destroy the Ukraine, which*

resulted in several million dead, of which two million were Catholic. This Church of the catacombs has its Diaspora, about two million people baptized around the world, especially in North America, Brazil, and Argentina, but also in Yugoslavia and Czechoslovakia. What was left in the Ukraine? It was not known. Rome had freed its Metropolite, Mgr Slipyj, who pleaded up to the time of his death for his Church. But the it remained underground and hunted down. And now it is rising again with all the force of its faith and resistance. This year, it has retrieved its churches and priests; and hundreds of Orthodox priests are joining it. It has contradicted the Marxist scientific diagnostic, its natural death in the Soviet paradise of a classless society. For lack of a spontaneous death, all the violence was beneficial in helping history which was on the wrong path - incarcerations, deportations, tortures, and brainwashing.

For me, the access to this paradise regained by witnesses of the faith was a difficult step, because this Church remains without a phone, fax machine, or means of communication. The post office did not deliver any of my letters, letters sent over a two-month period. It was an adventure to get there. To get to Lvov, you had to wait (each way) 24 hours in Kiev. And when I came back from the airport on November 29 at 8 o'clock in the morning, for a flight planned for 9:30 am, it instead left at 4 o'clock. Thus I arrived at night in Lvov (Lviv in Ukrainian), illiterate in this noble town where, in the end, nobody was waiting for me.

I was cursing my madness for undertaking this journey, and I was calling to the Heavens for help. Things then turned out all right. A rapid taxi driver offered his services, found my suitcase before I even saw it, took me to a hotel located almost across from the Greek-Catholic Cathedral that the Metropolite had just founded next to his palace. All of this canceled the need for previous problematic addresses and my plan to simply feel my way around. The wrinkles I had encountered were ironing out as if from a pocket handkerchief.

I discovered with amazement the admirable Ukrainian Baroque Cathedral, sparkling with gold and fervor - and, across from it, the Archbishop's palace, with its solemn double honor staircase made of gilded wrought iron. Here is the Metropolite, MGR Sterniuk (83 years old). A student at Louvain in 1931, he speaks French. But he was tired from his day as a young, hard-working octogenarian. We just exchanged a few words, and we made an appointment for the evening.

At 8 o'clock, I was again in front of the Archbishop, on the first floor of the beautiful palace, sparkling from mirrors and gilded moldings, with an inlaid hardwood floor. The Metropolite, modest, arrived in a simple belt-less black cassock, his face dominated by a limpid gaze and a small white beard.

R. Laurentin - Your Excellency, the journalist from the *Figaro-Magazine*, Visitor Loupan, met you last year in a small room where you had only room for your bed and the table you used as an altar. Only three people could squeeze in to hear mass. I can see that everything is changed in this vast archbishop's palace. What happened?

Mgr Sterniuk - It is true that last year I lived in this tiny room on 10A Tchkalova Street. In March, I got three rooms on the same street, and the Bishop's palace, which we had lost for 49 years, was just given back on November 21, 8 days ago.

R.L. - In good shape, as I can see.

S. - Not as good as you think. We had to clean piles of paper and garbage: eight days of cleaning that are just over. There were a few problems in keeping the main furniture which the inhabitants wanted to take with them.

As a result, the furniture was sparse, which contribute to giving the rooms this grandiose style.

R.L. - This terrestrial paradise, this Jerusalem, of which you must have dreamt during your captivity, did you get it back without too many problems?

S. - Mgr Colasuono (the ambassador of the Holy See in the East, since becoming Papal Nuncio in Moscow) came to take care of the final details on November 20. I was his interpreter. We had to establish when and how the rights conceded to the Orthodoxy would be out of date.

R.L. - Mgr Colasuono spoke in Italian?

S. - No, in French.

R.L. - How was your life during the 40-year period spent in the wilderness (1946-1987)?

S. - First I spent 5 years in jail - from 1947 to 1952. Then, I was sent back to my hometown, where I was given a job.

R.L. - What kind of work?

S. - Watching, cleaning, and sweeping city parks. I had to justify my life through work.

R.L. - Did it allow for a ministry?

S. - Yes, but underground, and carefully. After work, I visited one Christian family or another, to celebrate, to catechize, to baptize, and to hear confession.

R.L. - Always privately?

S. - Yes, and this method kept me from the traps of denunciation, because the families who received me for the sacrament were themselves compromised and motivated to keep the secret.

R.L. - Were there many arrests in 1946?

S. - All the Bishops were imprisoned. seven died. three have survived: the Metropolite Slipyj, the Bishop of Tcherneckyj, and an Auxiliary Bishop.

R.L. - And the priests?

S. - Two thirds were arrested.

R.L. - And lay people?

S. - Thousands were arrested. There were two million dead between 1946 and 1960.

This was the last period of Stalin's genocide. Stalin caused, since the thirties, the slaughter of 7 million Ukrainians.

R.L. - I have met in Toronto one of the lay people who was imprisoned for 23 years, Josyp Terelya.

S. - Yes, he fought and suffered, but he was damaged by his years spent in captivity - his health, a certain exaltation. When I saw him, he talked and talked, with enthusiasm, but without much order to it.

R.L. - This is a man who gave everything to God only, whole and disconcerting, like all prophets.

S. - Certainly, but the blows destroyed something in him.

R.L. - Are you happy with the new situation... with *perestroika*?

S. - What *perestroika*? It does not exist.

R.L. - There was glasnost, an opening, but without rebuilding (*perestroika*)?

S. - Of course we are happy for the freedom our Church recovered.

R.L. - In this new situation, how many Churches transferred to the Orthodoxy were given back to you?

S. - Almost all of them.

R.L. - But how many is that?

S. - There were 1200 Greek-Catholic Churches in 1946. About 1000 were given back to us, a tenth (so a hundred), being shared for an alternative cult, Orthodox and Greek-Catholic.

R.L. Did your faithful return to you?

S. - On this point, the situation is not as clear. After the suppression of our Church, many kept going to the church they were used to, managed by the Orthodoxy. But they did not receive any instruction, only the teaching on the liturgical signs, the sign of the cross, prayers to recite. Three quarters of the faithful to these churches turned Orthodox were Catholics. They spontaneously became Catholics again, without any problems.

R.L. - How many Orthodox became Catholic in the last two years?

S. - About 400.

R.L. - How many Greek-Catholics are there in the Ukraine?

S. - About 4 million, but there are almost 2 million in the rest of Russia, 500,000 in Poland, as many in Yugoslavia, 100,000 in Czechoslovakia, many in Canada, America, Argentina, and in Australia (30,000).

R.L. - Do you now have a Catholic press?

S. - Yes, I founded, this year, a bulletin of liaison this year.

R.L. - I was told that Cardinal Lubachivski (the quasi-Patriarchate, who resides in Rome) was going to come here.

S. - On March 30.

R.L. - Is he coming for a while or to reside here?

S. - He is coming. But is he to stay, I don't know.

I learned, by meeting, on the following day, Mgr Ivan Dacko, the Cardinal's secretary, that he was thinking of staying in Lvov, at the finally-recovered Archbishop's palace, which probably will become the Patriarchate.

R.L. - How many seminaries do you now have for the 5 million Catholic Ukrainians in the USSR?

S. - Two, with one here on the edge of Lvov.

R.L. - How many seminarians in Lvov?

S. - 350.

R.L. - And in the other seminary?

S. - In Stanislav? I don't know.

R.L. - What is this independent Orthodox Church that was recently created?

S. - It was founded in 1917-1918 by an Orthodox priest who was very pious and was afflicted by Russianization - Lypkinski. He wanted to establish a native Ukrainian Church. He founded that Church and tried to be ordained bishop. But since no Russian Bishop agreed, he had his ordination by the priests and the faithful from his community. It was not valid. This Church lasted 10 years. In 1931, Stalin annihilated it. The founder died in prison. In 1942, when the Germans occupied the Ukraine, a Ukrainian civil committee had the Minister of the cults, tied to the anti-Communist army of Petlora, ordained. They were beaten and driven out of the Ukraine. Finding shelter in Poland, they scattered. But their bishop had been validly ordained by the Orthodox Bishop of Warsaw. This Church was re-formed, a third time, by a priest who wanted to renew the Church outside of the Russian hierarchy, a native church within the frame of Ukrainian nationalism. He wrote to the Patriarchate of Constantinople to be recognized but did not receive an answer. He was validly ordained by the Orthodox Archbishop of Warsaw and proclaimed himself Patriarchate.

R.L. - This newborn group seemed important in number since in Kiev the government granted them three churches, but only one to the Greek-Catholics. And in Lvov itself, this Church recently landed from America, would have more churches than the Greek-Catholics who are yet on their own fief.

S. - They are not that numerous, and this group was encouraged to divide the Church by reinforcing nationalism.

Actually, the Native Church first rose up against the Russian Church. Its ultra-nationalism supports the Catholics reputed to be very Ukrainian but not political. It has a Patriarch, but the Russian Church reacted by giving the title Beatitude to the Russian Ukrainian Metropolite, and he will soon be Patriarch, or so it seems. As a result, the Greek-Catholic Metropolite should also soon be promoted to Patriarch, according to the wish formulated by the Council of Cardinal Slipyj, and renewed so many times since then.

As for the distribution of the churches planned for Kiev, it is not definitive. The Greek-Catholics hope for two churches, because they already have two parishes.

R.L. - And these apparitions in Grouchevo (Gruchiv) that are spoken of, what do you think of them.

S. - I do not believe them to be authentic.

R.L. - Why?

S. (with a smile) - The Blessed Virgin would not give money to the Communists!

R.L. - But she did not give any. People left money and the Communists took it (for their "peace work") as they took your Churches. I don't see the argument very well. Was there a theological and scientific examination of the young Maria Kyzin (the prophet)?

S. - No.

The Metropolite lives on faith and liturgy. The apparitions (which are always a secondary phenomenon in Christianity) are not part of his perspective, nor in his critical training received at Louvain. He seems to be afraid of them who draw the people in illumination.

R.L. - And the other apparitions talked about in the Ukraine?

S. - I also believe them false.

R.L. - Have you seen the prophets or had them studied.

S. - No.

R.L. - What are you waiting for from the West?

S. - That it support us with its authority, so that we can develop a truly spiritual Christian life in peace.

Josyp Terelya toward the end of his audience with John Paul II, after his expulsion from Russia, on the way to his exile in Toronto

Josyp Terelya with one of his children at the time of the interview on July 14, 1990

Boris Terelya, Josyp's brother, deceased on June 10, 1982, at the age of 38, after 16 years in prison.

JOSYP TERELYA

Confessor of faith in exile

On July 14 , 1990, I met a great witness of the Eastern Ukrainian Catholic Church in his exile home in Toronto, Josyp Terelya. This rebel from the underground church, born to Communist parents, was imprisoned 4 times in 23 years and 4 months, with sporadic releases from 1962 to 1987. A father of 3 children, he lived barely 3 years with his wife until his expulsion, on September 18, 1987, because such a witness was embarrassing, even for perestroika.

He tells of the secret life of the most persecuted Church under the Marxist regime - the Eastern Catholic Church, crushed (in the USSR as in Romania), not only by the atheist regime, but also by the Orthodox Church that had annexed it. These "Uniats", as they were called, are less supported than is Catholicism, because they are a thorn in the side of ecumenism.

Let's listen to Josyp Terelya talk about his life in this Church. In the following interview, he will speak of the

Blessed Virgin's apparitions in the Ukraine, to himself in his prison cell, in Gruchiv and elsewhere.

Rene Laurentin - Josyp Teryela, who are you?

Josyp Terelya - I was born in an old Ukrainian family, on October 27, 1943. My dad was a member of the Communist Party. During the war, soon after my birth, he was arrested in Czechoslovakia and detained in a concentration camp. He escaped to join Tito's army in Yugoslavia. Wounded in 1944, he was captured and sent to a concentration camp in Wiesbaden, then to Baden Baden. He was released by the American army, in which he served as interpreter, since he spoke 9 languages. Upon his return, he was immediately arrested. It was the time when all the people who were not for Stalin were repressed and killed. Liberated because of Tito's intervention, my father became head of the Communist Party of the region of Beskudes, in the center of the Carpathian Mountains. He was in charge of the fight against "Ukrainian bourgeois nationalism". But in 1951 (still under Stalin), he was again repressed, expelled from the Party, and sentenced. Another intervention from Tito saved him. I was being raised by my grandmother on my mother's side, Anna Sophia Fales, a fervent Catholic. I did know my parents until I was 12 years old.

Underground at age 6!

Around my grandmother, my whole family belonged to the Eastern Catholic Church, illegal since its suppression by Stalin - and clandestine. It was in 1949, at the age of 6, that I attended for the first time our liturgy from the catacombs. It was the first Sunday Russians confiscated our churches. Neighbors came to tell us that an underground priest (my mother's uncle, Dyonisius Drybidko) was going to celebrate Mass. He came at night. I was on watch and did my best not to fall asleep. But I was sleepy, and I was woke only when people were singing. Since that day, we gathered in the woods to celebrate the divine liturgy. I kept pictures (Here's one taken in the woods by Ivan Matgitych, Ukrainian Catholic bishop in the Carpathian Mountains).

Underground School

At 14, I joined the *Catholic Action* in the Isusovci group, which renewed the *Confraternity of the Sacred Heart of Jesus*. The goal was to restore the cult of the Sacred Heart and the Eucharist for the youth. Women were already very active. We wanted to mobilize the young and adult males.

In 1960, we held a meeting with more than a thousand participants, in order to celebrate the Eucharist. Our lectures, seminars and discussions ended with the Lord's Supper. Our meetings were held in big private houses. We had to be on our guard, as the Soviets organized night raids. The KGB had its informers; they were betraying us then.

Mass always ended our meetings. The participants sat around the table. After Mass we set out bread with peas, salt and oil. That was our meal. We prayed together.

Young activists, between 6 and 16 years old, read a text from the Gospel; and we applied it to our life and our times. This is how we developed our Catholic responsibility. Our purpose was not just to preserve the Church or to hear mass. No. We engaged in discussions with Jehovah's Witnesses and Pentacostals. Russians were financing the underground Protestant group against the Catholic Church.

Thanks to this formation, at age 14 a young Catholic knew and understood the symbols of faith. He knew why he was a Christian. And I am surprised that here, in the West, so few know their *Creed* and who Jesus is. They think one can go to any other Church. But we are the true Apostolic Church, the

Church that comes from Jesus and was founded on Jesus. Thus we can not engage in compromise with those who call themselves Christians, but have abandoned the Catholic faith. I have often been asked how I understand ecumenism. My understanding of ecumenism is Catholic, [I recognize] people from another faith or rite, when they love Jesus with all their heart. But I must add that loving Jesus Christ is not enough. We must obey him, and we often forget this. There even are priests who call on us to love Jesus but forget to tell us that we must also obey him. We have trained our youth. That is how I was taught. In the matter of ecumenism, anyone who truly receives Jesus Christ, is baptized according to the rites of the Church, and accepts the Catholic faith according to its foundations, is ecumenical: he truly belongs to God. Ecumenism can only be one, or else it is not ecumenism.

My cousins were repressed; my uncles imprisoned. They were priests.

I lived with my parents until I was 19. I was then finishing my engineering studies in construction. Then I looked for work in Kiev, where I met my future wife, Olena, a student at the Medical Institute. But from then on I was hardly ever out of prison for 23 years and 4 months, in 4 episodes.

My prisons

Some circles present me as a defender of Catholics only. It is not true. It was us Catholics who raised our voice, but for the defense of all religious groups in the Ukrainian territory, Orthodox and Protestants. I have often been asked why I, a Catholic, defended Orthodox and Protestants, because they never said a word on our behalf. It is they who must answer.

At 19, I was arrested for the first time and sentenced to 4 years of internment in a work camp. It was my first arrest. I was released after 5 years. On my return, in July 1976, I married Olena. She was 34 and I was 33. I was not free for very long: only one year.

I was again arrested in 1978, this time in secret confinement in the prison of Detrvskniprop, for 3 years, then in others, for a year and a half. After that, I was freed in 1982, but not for long.

In fact I had created a group in order to obtain the legalization of the Church. We pursued this goal without trespassing the limits set by the Constitution of the USSR. Our position was as follows: according to the Russian Constitution, Article 52, there is no Ukrainian Constitution. Thus we do not possess in our own right. They took our churches; they are not giving them back today. According to the Russian constitution: "IN THE Socialist Union, there is not and there cannot be a forbidden religion."

It is on these foundations that we started our *Movement for the legislation in 1982*. I was arrested, that same year, in December. They kept me until 1983. After I served my sentence, the camp authorities did not free me.

R.L. - Why?

J.T - We don't know! They did not know what to do with me.

I protested: "I am now detained illegally! I should have been freed yesterday!"

"We don't know anything about it!"

They put me in a neutral section of the camp which only the guards could enter. I stayed there until my wife came. It is she who got me out.

In 1984, 14 days after my liberation, we started publishing the *Chronicles of the Ukrainian Catholic Church.*

So far nothing has changed for Ukrainian Catholics. I was president of the group to which belonged a monk, Brother Gregory Budzinslyj; a faithful woman, Stephania Petrash Sichko, still with me for better or worse. With them were two others, as well as my wife Olena, and a fourth person I cannot name, even today. We do not yet have, in the USSR, a *perestroika* that allows us to speak freely.

I was arrested again, one year and four months later, in 1985. The country tribunal sentenced me to 12 years in prison. Until then, I had been detained in all sorts of jails, some better, others worse. But the camps in the regions of Perm were something terrible. I was never allowed to leave my solitary confinement. Prisoners were beaten until they lost consciousness and without the events that developed in Western Europe in 1987, I would not be with you today.

During this period, many were killed, Oleska Tychyj, and Jurij Lytwyn. The last victim was Slavko Pushkar, after my liberation. This Ukrainian fellow countryman from the Carpatians Mountains, officer in the Russian Army, sent as an instructor in the Korean Army, was accused of spying for North Korea. He was sentenced to 15 years in prison, then executed.

I was freed from the camp of Perm on February 5, 1987. I started work right away. I started collecting signatures for the dismantlement of nuclear plants in the Ukraine. I was taking signatures in the woods, at night, in Zarvanytsia. These petitions against nuclear plants had started on April 26, 1986, on the day of the first explosion at Chernobyl, at dawn, around 5 o'clock in the morning. Nobody paid attention. A few monks understood from having studied the *Apocalypse* according to Saint John the Evangelist, in which Chernobyl is expressly mentioned. The Apostle speaks of the "*absynthe* star that burned like a torch and spoiled a third of the water for the death of many men" (AP 8, 10-11). In our languages, *absynthe* is *Chernobyl!*

In September 1987, I was expelled from Russia. I met the Pope in Rome. His first question was "How is your wife doing, how are your children doing? How did they live when you were in prison?"

I had a 43-minute audience with the Holy Father. Nobody else was present. I hope to go back to Rome in Autumn (1990), if I can finally obtain a visa.

The illusions of perestroika

R.L. - But how is your country today, with *perestroika?*

J.T. - There are still many lies. Russians say that Raoul Wallenberg died in 1947. It's not true. Believe me. I saw Raoul Wallenberg in 1970, in the prison of Vladimir. He was still alive. In 1985, we knew which cell he was detained in. We must pray for this man. I regret that so many Jews, gone out of the Soviet Union in such a large immigration, remain quiet about Wallenberg. They should redouble their efforts and demands. The officer who questioned Wallenberg is still alive. At one point, he wanted to give a press conference. But he was threatened with imprisonment. We stopped his action. We must remember these events, not for vengeance, but to convert. It is better to have a tomorrow with Gorbachev, and all those who have persecuted and tortured me all my life.

Persecution

The Russians tried 8 times to make me sign a declaration which said I rallied the Russian Orthodox Holy Mother Church, and 8 times I refused to sign.

R.L. - Where does the persecution stand?

J.T. - Until now, nothing has changed for the Catholic Ukrainians. Last June (1989), Jaroslaw, who was a prisoner with me for many long years, celebrated in secrecy the mass for which I have the picture. It had been organized by the young *Catholic Action*. There were 20 or 30,000 boys and girls for this mass. Some Orthodox brothers had joined in to ask for the legalization of the Ukrainian Catholic Church in the Soviet Union.

It is difficult to make people, who do not know the Soviet Union understand that we are still forced to celebrate in the woods and forests. As long as we were underground, we were illegal. But when we started coming out of the catacombs and celebrating openly, the persecutions quickly forced us to return to the woods.

During Gorbachev's *perestroika*, we were more perse- cuted than under Stalin. But our action had its outcome, which is that now we do it legally. They fine us, they throw us in jail; but despite all that our protestation is legal. The people see what we do.

You have no idea about the persecutions the Catholic Church suffered from. Not only were we beaten and perse- cuted, but we were without bread, kept from buying butter for our children, because it is a big problem today to find cream, cheese and butter. It takes long lines, and sugar is rationed; and all this time the USSR proclaims to the world that its social system is the best and that its country is the richest.

Often, I am asked, Satan, is he in the Soviet Union? It's absurd. Satan is everywhere. Today, the world is dominated by Satan. Not only the Communist regime (Gottwald in Czechoslovakia, Stalin in Russia, Tito in Yugoslavia). No, in the whole world: America, Portugal, Italy, USSR, you can find Satan everywhere, you can find the decline of faith everywhere, a proliferation of abortions. There is nothing worse than abortion, and nobody is worried. Mothers kill their own children. Why? Because their governments and their countries have forgotten that it is murder.

R.L. - Did you go to prison because you were Catholic or because you were a revolutionary?

J.T. - As a Catholic! But I am a revolutionary Catholic and I caused changes nobody dare dreams of. I organized the legal Catholic movement in the USSR: ten years of intense work with God. And were out of the catacombs. It was a gift from God.

R.L. - Those who are in the gulags, are they kept on political or religious grounds?

J.T. - Fundamentally, it is because of their nationalism that they are persecuted by the Russians. In the camps and the prisons, there are very few Russians, but many dissidents, those who fight against Russians for the independence of Lithuania, Estonia, Georgia, Armenia, Azerbaidjan, Kazakhstan - all for liberty. These captive nations fight for the independence of their region.

R.L. - Are there only Catholics, or Orthodox also?

J.T. - Almost no Orthodox. Out of 10,000 prisoners where I was, not one Orthodox, but there were some Protestants.

R.L. - Were there Jews and Moslems?

J.T. - There were Jews in small numbers; generally, not for religious reasons, but because they wanted to leave Russia - those who are called *refuseniks*. During the 20 years I spent in prison, I may have met 5 or 6 Jews imprisoned on religious grounds in all the camps I went to, all through Russia.

R.L. - What is the life of a gulag?

J.T. - Not always the same, and it is difficult to answer in a few words. A prison is a prison. A concentration camp is a concentration camp. But it does not mean we did not do anything. We preached, even the officers and the KGB.

R.L. - It said that the situation got better with *perestroika?*

J.T. - It's very relative. Up till now nothing has fundamentally changed in Russia. I repeat it one more time, in the time of *glasnost* and *perestroika*, the greatest pressures are exerted against Ukrainian Catholics, against our political and national life. The world does not understand that Gorbachev's Communist regime's only purpose is to strengthen the Communist system. The sole goal of *perestroika* is not to put an end to the Communist system, but to consolidate it. What happens in the Soviet Union is not the will of Gorbachev, but the fruit of our effort. We have started to raise our voice to mobilize people. Today, it has become impossible to kill somebody. The KGB tries to control all these religious and national movements. We'll see if they succeed. But Russia can no longer go back to mass murders like under Stalin. They will still be sacrifices, they will fire at us. They will throw us into their prisons and their camps. They still do it today. The system of concentration camps still exists in the Soviet Russia. If Gorbachev talks of *perestroika*, why doesn't he root out the cause of its evils - the Communist system? Those who adore the beast wear its mark on their forehead (he makes allusion to the *Apocalipse* 14:9 and 20:4 which he applies to Gorbachev's birthmark, an apocalyptic consideration which is his responsibility). Gorbachev should abolish Communism and stop the repression of the people. He should allow the free expression of religious faith, because religious faith does not only mean freedom to pray, but also to spread and teach the Gospel. Then it would be a true *perestroika*. I am experienced, 30 years of activity in the Catholic Church. Everything that is not built in the name of God will fail. What is built in the name of God will remain. The Ukraine will be one of the strongest European nations in a Christian Europe. When the Ukraine becomes a great nation, there will be peace, a real peace; and the whole world will be converted. Our life was hard. Russia tried to destroy our identity for two centuries. There was no difference between the Communists and the Tsar. It is the same! Russian Tsars and Russian Communists destroyed us and continue to destroy us. But the Mother of God watches over us, and what she said will be.

R.L. - What do you think of Gorbachev's visit to the Pope?

J.T. - I'm skeptical, because Gorbachev comes with one purpose: to deceive the world by showing that the Communists speak to the Pope. But it's all a bluff. It is pure propaganda. What Gorbachev wants is more money and more technology.

R.L. - The pictures show that churches are full in the Soviet Union.

J.T. - Yes, but they are Ukrainians. In the Soviet Union, the Russian Orthodox Church is 82% Ukrainian. The rest (18%) is in Bielorussia, Russia and Romania.

R.L. What do you think of Solzhenitsyn?

J.T. - He described Russia as it is. He is RUSSIAN. He did not say anything new. It was known before him and it had already been written on. Soljenitsyne caught the wave of propaganda that was rising in the West. But Soljenitsyne must be respected as someone who dared expose the truth about the Soviet Union, not only Russians, but nations and people.

R.L. - What do you think you will tell us in the future?

J.T. - There will be great changes in Central Europe, not because of Gorbachev and President Bush, but *because of the people who pray and the youth. On September 20, 1989, we heard that the General Secretary of the Communist Party in the Ukraine was ousted from power. It is the fruit of people's sacrifice. These changes will spread to Central Europe and the Soviet Union. We will have the independence of the Baltic Countries, an independent Byeloiussia, a Ukraine, a Georgia, and an independent Russia. This independence will be built upon the truth from the Gospel. We are still suffering. Gorbachev threatens not to give liberty to these people, but it doesn't depend on Gorbachev. If Russia wants to be respected by other nations, it must give independence to all these people. As long as Russia continues to dominate all these nations, dialogue and justice will not be possible. Where there is no justice, there is no peace. God calls for peace and tranquility. Peace and tranquility will come from justice and not from the General Secretary of the Communist Party. He will do many things he is opposed to. At the end of September 1989, he said on te*levision that he would not give freedom to the Baltic States or the Ukraine. He will soon say something completely different. I believe that we will see great changes in the world.

In 1987, Bishop Paulo Wasylyk personally converted Lutheran parishes in Estonia, by preaching. These parishioners and their pastor became Greek-Catholics.

We must take our hat off when we pass in front of a church; we must make the sign of the cross when we pass in front of a crucifix. We must testify for Jesus Christ in front of all. If we were to give a true testimony to Jesus Christ, there would be a mass conversion; and then we would possess this peace the Mother of God urges us to obtain.

We can do it. It will come. And then you will remember my words in your countries where faith diminishes.

Here is Josyp Terelya's personal testimony on his underground and persecuted action. He speaks bluntly, without tact or nuance. He has that right, he who never compromised with the enemy, even near death.

In a second interview, he will testify on the Blessed Virgin's apparitions (Ukraine). He saw her in Gruchiv, shortly after his last liberation (1987) and recognized the one who appeared to him once, during his 23 years in prison, and saved his life when he was dying of cold.

3

Apparitions in Ukraine

JOSYP TERELYA's testimony

In the early editions of my book <u>Multiplications of the Blessed Virgin's apparitions</u> *today[1], I was very reserved about the Gruchiv (Russian - Gruchevo) apparitions in the Ukraine[2]. I had collected the following information: on April 26, 1987, the anniversary of Chernobyl, Marina Kizyn, age 12, leaves for mass. She sees on the balcony of the chapel, 200 meters below her house, a woman dressed in black with a child in her arms. She tells her mom who reasons with her... but finally sees the same thing and kneels. People talk about it. People come, surge to the place, soon from all of the USSR, from the Baltic States to Georgia.*

The study of a voluminous document file had left me perplexed because the testimonies differed. Some even said that the Blessed Virgin had appeared on television or on some Party building. Reserve was imperative.

Without clarifying everything, Josyp Teryela's direct and fiery testimony left an impression on me. He had already seen his first apparition of the Blessed Virgin in February 1972 in his terrible prison at Vallenberger.

Josyp Terelya - I was then in secret confinement. The room was freezing, I was hurting from head to toe. A lamp was burning in my cell. I took off the muff and warmed up my hands. But the guard saw me through the spy hole; he turned the light off. In 10 minutes I was petrified by the cold. My lips could not open anymore. I was still conscious, but I could not move a limb. I was lying on the bed. It was then that I felt the warm contact of a woman's hand, soft like cream. I was warmed. I felt the warmth in the room. I thought I was hallucinating or dying. But then I heard the voice:

"You called me and I came to you. You do not believe it is me?"

Then I saw a young woman in front of me; it was Her, for the first time!

In all, I saw the Mother of God seven times - once in prison, then six times in Gruchiv. I did not see her hair. Her head was covered with a veil. That first time, she told me:

"You will not be freed from this prison, you have only been part of the way. But do not be afraid, I am with you."

Investigations and intimidations

I got up and started walking. I was warm. I took off my shirt and stayed with only my underwear on. The guard was looking through the spy hole, stunned. KGB officers came in, dressed in their heavy coats and fur hats. The room was cold; the walls were covered with ice. The doctor, a woman, examined me and shrugged her shoulders: "You have lost your mind!" But the following days, doctors came from Moscow. They were surprised that I was not frozen. They did not hide it: "You should have died of cold."

What they wanted to know was why my body was warm:

"There are techniques to stimulate blood flow. He does yoga," the KGB said.

"That's absurd," the doctors said. "Yoga cannot do anything."

Anyway, I should have been frozen. Only the woman doctor believed me. Today she has become Catholic. She is the only one who really talked to me.

General Lunz, chief psychiatrist, came to interrogate me.

"Very well, Terelya, we know you are a fanatic believer. We want to know what means you use to overcome these freezing temperatures. What is the system you use to prevent freezing? Yoga?"

I answered,

"I saw the Mother of God. I'm telling you I saw her!"

I was kept away from all the other prisoners. They kept me in prison for another half a year. They did not free me.

The Mother of God's prophecy was accomplished to the last detail, including this latest liberation.

Colonel Vynogradov said:

"If we free him, the event will be known by all the fanatics. We cannot release him."

I wrote some verses, and I was sentenced again for these verses, thus not released.

A month later, I was transferred to Yefortovo, at the Serbsky Institute. They put me through psychiatric tests. Many tests! General Lunz, Professor Taitze, and Academician Snizhnevsky told me,

"Come on! Why are you so stubborn? Deny that you saw the Mother of God, and go home. Our conclusions will determine what we'll do with you. Help us!"

Professor Taitze questioned me:

"Do you believe that the Mother of God was conceived immaculate, and immaculate, gave birth to Jesus?"

I refused to answer this provocative question.

"That's enough to declare you psychologically abnormal!" the woman doctor said.

She added,

"Did you study biology in school?"

"Yes," I answered.

"You know how cells are formed; you know what a spermatozoid is. Then you must deny that a child could be conceived and born just from his mother."

"No, I don't deny it. That's how people are born, but God was not born that way. He is not a man."

She said:

"Think about it carefully; your future hangs on your answer."

They declared me psychologically unbalanced.

"We will treat you until you forget your God!"

I was in a conference room, with 250 psychiatrists from the Serbsky Institute. Academician Snizhnevsky, Lieutenant General Moronov, the director of the Serbsky Institute, General Lunz, Professor Taitze and his wife. All the leading luminaries were there, and I told them that not one hair would come off my head.

"I will not take one pill or one gram of your medications. You have nothing to do with me!" I declared.

"We'll see", they answered.

Thank God, the Mother of God kept watch over me during the three years I was kept in this psychiatric institute. They did not give me one pill. It was not a miracle, but it became unexplainable, because I had been locked up there to be beaten, to be killed by tranquilizers and neuroleptics. The doctors were angry with me. There were times when the KGB intervened on my behalf, and they did not force me to take their medications.

Lights in the night

Let's go back to May 9, 1987, when, after thinking, I left for Gruchiv. I went believing I would not see anything...

But when I arrived, we saw a strange light. I could not describe it. It was as if it had come from another planet. It was dark and the light could be seen from far away. It was so light that you could have seen a needle. It was not the light of day, nor the light of night. And in this light, I saw Her like I see you. I wanted to reach for Her, to touch Her. I felt Her and I was able to touch Her. At the same time, I was talking to others who were there. There was a great peaceful atmosphere. People were illuminated. The leaves from the trees shed light. Everything was as electrified, bathed in this light that united all those who were there.

There were a lot of people. It was before dawn. A mass of people were already assembled when I arrived. I stayed there until the 12th of May. A cinema crew from Moscow was there. A Russian woman cried out:

"I cannot understand what is happening. I must write an article, but I cannot write I too saw the Mother of God!"

I have often been asked: "What did the Mother of God say, how did she speak?" I would not call those "visions". Visions are hallucinations. No, they were not visions, it's incorrect to call them so. It was the Mother of God alive, it was a woman alive. She talked with us. Her face was full of life. Everybody saw her. I saw her, and others saw her with me. And we did not just see her, we heard her. Some heard one thing, others another. When the Mother of God turned towards us, she spoke to each one. There are some things I don't reveal to anybody because of certain reasons. When I will finish my book, everything will be published. This is what I can reveal now.

When the Mother of God spoke (I think I hear her voice, even today), she started by saying:

"My daughter, Ukraine my daughter, I came to you!"

These are the same words she had addressed to the Ukraine, in Seredne, a century after the apparitions in Lourdes, on December 22, 1954, in the mountains. She had then said,

"Ukraine my daughter, I came to you; you are the one most enslaved. You are the one who suffered the most for your faith in Christ. I came to you."

This she repeated in Gruchiv, which is a complement and an accomplishment of Fatima, because if Russia does not convert to Christ-the-King, World War III will be unavoidable: the Mother of God told Fatima.

When she spoke, there were about 52,000 of us. You cannot imagine this crowd. We did an estimation. Many Jews were converted on that day. Many of those who were there did not even know how to make the sign of the cross, but they were converted, and they proclaimed it. They asked for our help. They did not know us and we did not know them. They were from Moscow, and did not know what Orthodoxy or Catholicism were. But what they saw, what they experienced is what we all saw - the Mother of God. They did not come with the idea to see her, but only for a pilgrimage, to pray. Adults saw her, children saw her. All the children saw her.

Some saw the shining cross. Others heard a voice, but did not see anything. This confirms that the Mother of God came for those who needed her, and how they needed her. We said the rosary, without interruption, for 24 hours. When one group was finished, another started.

I have often been asked: "How did you hear her voice?" It was not a hallucination or a mass psychosis. When I looked upon the Mother of God, she was looking at me with her eyes. She looked at each person with her eyes. How would it be possible if it was a hallucination? The people saw a woman alive. Some saw her in a flamboyant robe, other in a white robe. As for me, I saw her three times with a flamboyant robe. Her face was clear and white - the face of an 18- to 20-year-old young woman. Very beautiful, charming. It was not a natural beauty, but an indescribable beauty.

She asked us to pray, to teach the prayers to the children, the rosary; to constantly pray for the dead, those who were killed; because if a Christian forgets the dead, he who does not pray for them is a very poor Christian. She asked us to convert the non-believers, to work among them.

On May 12, the Mother of God spoke again. I heard these words:

"I came to you, because here the people are fervent, and this fervent people will spread my words everywhere. I know where I must go. I am going where it is the best for my Son."

But why did she come to Gruchiv? The Mother of God answered that question. She did not come to Moscow, but to this fervent people. If she had appeared to non-believers, they would have been frightened and would have not said anything. The Mother of God comes where she is welcome, where she is needed. The fervent people that came to Gruchiv has spread the news everywhere in the Soviet Union. Some came from the other end of Russia: Ostravasakalina, 14,000 kilometers from there. They had come to prostrate themselves and pray before the Mother of God. Many of them did not know how to pray yet. They did not know the *Lord's Prayer*. They did not know the *Credo*. They did not know the *Hail, Mary*. There, they learned to pray and became Catholic.

I was a witness to the coming of a Russian Orthodox priest.

"This is all Uniat Catholic propaganda," he said. "I want to see this Terelya. Where is he?"

I was there,

; I was preaching, I had been talking for five hours. People were asking me,

"Josyp, did you memorize that? How do you know all that?"

I must confess that I did not really know where I got these words. I did not even know what I was saying. All the words came, very simply, as they were coming to me. *Since the time when they had wanted me to die of cold, the Mother of God remained with me.*

The divine liturgy was celebrated without interruption in Gruchiv. I have pictures. I stayed there until May 18, 1987.

A constellation of apparitions

After Gruchiv, there were 13 other apparitions, 14 total, in the Ukraine.

R.L. - Are the apparitions still happening in the Ukraine?

J.T. - Some say that they stopped when the Russian Orthodox Church took possession of the Church. That's not true. The non-believers who say that. To say that the Mother of God appeared only for the Catholics is not true. The Mother of God appeared to each one. She said many times, - You are not at peace. You want everything and now, convert everyone to my Son. Only those who have and understand love will convert. Do penance and pacify your heart. You are full of fear and apprehension. You will see what will come. It is almost impossible to prevent. If the people do not accept the Christ-King; then there will be war, the air will be on fire, water will evaporate, even the air will burn. There will be a great fire. I see that fire, the village burning, the water burning, in flames. Just from thinking about it my whole body is sweating, charged with electricity, and my hands are numb, this is what I feel while talking to you.

Healings occurred, leukemics in particular. They went home completely healed. The Soviet press talks about it. The doctors are embarrassed.

Lately, the Mother of God has appeared dressed in black.

To me, she spoke in Ukrainian.

Sometimes, I wonder what language she speaks, because over there are Russians, Georgians, etc., and all hear the same message in their own tongue. What does it mean? Is it a translation? It is beyond our little minds. We can only understand one thing; we must believe, pray, and change our lives. The Mother of God tells us to offer our lives. After the original sin, sacrifice is the principal law for each one. Remember that sin is the forbidden pleasure; the Blessed Virgin talked a lot about it:

"Each one of you must take part in the sufferings of Jesus; that is how you will redeem those who have sinned, do not doubt it. Do not be afraid and pray; pray all the time. Recognize Jesus publicly; do not be ashamed of making the sign of the cross. Prepare for great persecutions and new sacrifices."

How many not really committed Christians do not dare to bow when passing in front of a church! We must testify without shame, cross ourselves when our bus passes in front of a church. We must convert everyone.

Great things have started. In the Philippines, Catholics went down in the streets to face the troops without one soldier firing. There will be a time when the Mother of God will do the same in the Soviet Union; not one soldier will fire. All the divisions will pass. It will be a great rebirth. Only what God does will remain.

The Mother of God said that the Ukraine will become independent in the next ten years. And this will be. Remember what I told you two years ago. It is all confirmed. Recent events have confirmed it.

Pray for the Pope, that he perform a new consecration of Russia. On May 14, the Mother of God said;

"Pray often in community. What is difficult is worth the trouble. You have doubts that trouble you. You hope for help

113

from far away. You will not receive such help. Help comes only from my Son. A long, sad road awaits you. And along the way you will find friends, those who are always with my Son. I will not abandon you. But act on your own! Do not worry, do not be full of anger; you are often angry because of your pride and human vanity. Pray, and prayers, the rosary, will save you. The Antichrist does everything to break you. Remember; peace only come from Redemption. Peace is calm and rest, and you are not yet in peace."

50% of my family was killed by Fascists, Hungarian and German. Another part, by Russians, when they came. But I have no resentment towards Russians, neither towards Germans or Hungarians. Each destroyed us. The destiny of the Ukraine is horrible. Each occupying force that came into our country did something new to destroy us. Here's a picture from 1939 Hungarians executing officers and soldiers from the Ukrainian Republic of the Carpathian Mountains. Let's not forget our dead; lets pray for the criminals. Look at them in this picture. They were laughing. It's sick, these people who kill others and laugh. You have to have fallen low to become a non-believer, without God, to kill a person and laugh!.

In July 1989, Patriach Pimene sent eleven Orthodox priests to Gruchiv for anti-Catholic propaganda. Five of them became Catholic on the third day. They left the Orthodox Church. Six priests converted in one month, and all are now Catholic.

In the crowd of Gruchiv, I had pushed through to make my way. I saw KGB officers who knew me. They thought I was there with an official authorization. I called them: "What are you doing here?" They left immediately. They did not want to talk to me. My future was already sealed. It had been decided that I should be expelled from the country. They had already prepared a foreign passport. I did not know anything about it then. They did not want to say anything to me. That day, there were 40 cars from Georgia. They thought I was in prison. They started to say, "Josyp is here." They made room for me. When I got to the middle, I saw that piles of money had already been thrown on the ground. I raised my hands and proclaimed,

"Money will not save you. The Mother of God does not need your money, she wants your prayers. Say the rosary for those who are in prison and in the concentration camps."

We kneeled and started saying the rosary. There were about 200 KGB and militia officers. The officers kneeled and took off their caps. We said the rosary, we meditated for about 4 hours. When it was over, I got up to leave and approached one of the officers, Major Mikael Tarakhowych. I told him:

"Why did you kneel? You are atheist, you are Communist..."

He said:

"Listen, if I had not kneeled, the people would have cast a spell over us. You do not believe what is happening here?"

They had kneeled without wanting to, they had to. One of the officers, a middle-aged Lieutenant, saw the Mother of God - an atheist, a Communist who had never prayed. He was troubled. He took his revolver and fired and immediately fell to the ground; his arm became as black as if he had received an electric shock.

People say he died. It's not true, he came around a little bit later. But by then, he looked like he had been electrocuted.

A similar episode occurred. A KGB officer from the detail of Lvov looked for a young militiaman and told him:

115

"Why do you allow the people to come see a miracle?"

The poor man raised his hands:

''What, what can I do when I myself see the Mother of God?"

The militia then tore off his uniform and his epaulettes. They were red with anger. He was put in a psychiatric prison for a week, then released. Now he works actively for the Catholic Church. It is the work of the Mother of God.

There were many other apparitions in the Ukraine. In Zarvanytsia Hoshiw, in all the sanctuaries and monasteries the Russians destroyed in the last 40 ycars, - in all these places, there were apparitions of the Mother of God.

In Zarvanytsia, she appeared in 1987, 1988, and 1989. She has often appeared to people. She talks to them; she warns them.

I prefer the testimonies from the simple people, workers and farmers, because they write without artifice, while intellectuals always add something from themselves. I have thousands of letters.

The difference is that in Gruchiv, she appears regularly and not occasionally. That is why this is where the people go especially to see her and hear her repeat what she has already said on the mountain of Seredne.

The Mother of God said in Gruchiv a lot of things she said in Medjugorje. I follow closely the events of Medjugorje; it is almost the same message. She mentioned Medjugorje in Gruchiv in 1987, but the Ukrainian people know little about Medjugorje. It is in Gruchiv that they heard that name.

This being said, the Mother of God asked us to say the rosary every night at 7 o'clock with the children and all of the people. Since then, we have formed large prayer groups in all of the Ukraine, and we pray all the time. Now, in Toronto, I have lost contact. I keep this presence. It's only my testimony. The Church will judge.

One can be surprised by such wonders. It takes one's breath away. One day, history will have to verify what Josyp Terelya and others say about these apparitions. Meanwhile, Josyp Terelya is an eye witness. This witness has paid a great price for his confession of faith. On several points, he shows a critical mind. His testimony carries weight and deserves respect.

Setting, History and Background of Gruchiv

During the War of Bodhan Khmelnytsky with the kings of Poland in the 17th century, the Virgin Mary appeared where the Chapel of Gruchiv stands today. The people planted a willow to commemorate the event instead of the apparition. At the end of the 18th century, and the beginning of the 19th century, a spring of clear water appeared at the foot of the willow. People from the surrounding village came to take the water for their various illnesses and the fame spread beyond Galicia's borders. In 1806, the villagers placed an icon of the Virgin Mary on the willow; the icon was painted that year by Stephan Chapowskyj. They often gathered there to pray; they offered votive candles; they celebrated in honor of the Virgin Mary. That did not please the owners and administrators of the property. They decided to stop these pilgrimages. The owners hired a non-believer, Justin Kina, to build a fence around the willow, but the whole Kina family died soon after.

In 1856, a cholera epidemic spread in the village, killing many inhabitants of that region. A woman had a dream: she saw the Mother of God who said to her, "My daughter, I ask you to clean the desecrated well, celebrate mass there, and death will cease in the village."

The people gathered on the village square. They came to the wells with their tools; and true to the promise, cholera disappeared from the village when the request was accomplished. People bought that well the owners and built a chapel around the wells. The Church was consecrated by the village priest, Brother Klychevych, with five other priests. The chapel was consecrated to the Holy Trinity, because that people had seen three candles burning in the well.

22 years later (1878), the chapel was remodeled and rebuilt. That new Church is the one that has remained up to this day. It was dedicated on June 2, 1878, by the village priest, Brother Ivan Kostenskyj. An iconostasis was erected in 1883, and frescoes painted on the walls. The Church was again blessed by Mgr Ivan Wojtovich, on August 27, 1901, during the feast of the Assumption according to the Julian calendar.

Bishop Constantin Chekhovych issued a decree, with the authorization from the Holy See, giving complete indulgence to those who would visit this sanctuary according to the habitual norms of the Church.

4

INVESTIGATION AT GRUCHIV

The Chapel in Gruchiv, seen from the village above

The divergent files on Gruchiv that had been put together left me puzzled. Josyp Terelya's direct and fiery testimony had made an impression on me. He manifested the prophetic sincerity and extent of the popular faith movement which reappeared suddenly at the dawn of *glasnost*. He left many points open for criticism. And the Metropolite of Sterniuk, from Lvov, like the one from Paris, was reserved, not because of an investigation, but because of his critical rigor.

It was not easy. At the hotel, a charming interpreter who spoke French helped me with practical questions, but she was not encouraging for Gruchiv.

"Taxis are few. But you could use the car from the hotel. But it's expensive."

"How much would it be?"

"At least 200 dollars."

"See if it's possible."

"Yes, but we will also have to seek authorization from the authorities; and they discourage trips to Gruchiv, it seems to me."

Decidedly, I had little chance of success.

At the Archbishop's Palace, the meeting with the Metropolite was not any more encouraging, as we have seen (p. 80). Taught at Louvain, he has a critical mind and little sympathy for these apparitions and evidently does not encourage me to go there. I tell him my intentions.

"I don't have any a prior ideas, but I haven't made head nor tails of it for several years. I would like to find out. In order to discern, there is no other means than to see the people, the places, the atmosphere."

He did not see any problem with this. On top of that, I met Nadia Dzera again, the interpreter who had kindly helped me in this Archbishop's Palace, where nobody speaks any of the languages I know... except for the Metropolite. I asked her about the possibility of finding a taxi to go to Gruchiv - maybe a Christian who could translate Ukrainian. She seemed encouraging. She was going to take care of it: tomorrow, November 30, being the only possible day.

"Call me at 7:00 a.m.," she said.

As a precaution, I start calling at 9:00 p.m., to see if the number was operational. I have already had so many surprises with Russian phones. Luckily, it worked! She had already paved the way; she would be there tomorrow at 10 o'clock with a car. She had arranged for an hour off work to help me. Her English was very clear.

The next day, right at 10 o'clock, she is there with the car. She warns me about the negotiated price:

"50 dollars, okay?"

It did sound like a lot here. With the fall of the dollar, it's only 200 francs. It would be 5 to 10 times more in France for this 60-kilometer ride.

So here we are on the road crossed by long dense lines of cars and trucks. We move slowly, with stops at each gas station that looks open, even if there is a line, since the tank is low. But, every time, we are without success.

Between industrial cities, there is the countryside, very crowded in the immense plain of black lands, that make the side road extremely muddy. The ground is black, but the wayside crosses are flowered under the November mist.

Around 11:30 a.m., I see a small chapel at the end of the road. The site is very different from what I had imagined from several drawings and bad photographs. Reality is always pretty different from what we dream. But I do recognize the building - the wooden chapel, the central dome and two little wings with a modest roof, at the bottom of a gently sloped hill, lined with houses. The one on top, on the left, is Maria Kazin's, 200 meters beyond the chapel. While leaving this house to go to Sunday mass, she saw the Blessed Virgin for the first time, above the chapel balcony.

Before climbing the hill, we speak with an energetic and friendly old farm woman. She has the key to the chapel. While she looks for it, we go up to the Kysins. No luck, the house is locked up. I take a photograph of the house for lack of anything better and than the chapel seen from where I stand. I admire the well, with its large wheel to turn the pulley. But the well is closed, The photograph would not turn out, and the misty weather changes my mind.

Another farm woman helps us. The grapevine works well in the village, and people start to conglomerate. I am right away informed,

"The parents are working and the daughter is at school."

It does not disconcert the dynamic interpreter. She herself is a teacher and director of studies in Lvov. She is at home in a school, a nice village school that spreads out lengthwise, single storied, between the trees. Children appear to be in recess. Nadia goes in the school as if she were at home. And soon Maria Kizyn appears, modest in a school girl smock, shy, but simple, docile and without fuss. She is accompanied by an older friend, and Nadia gently makes her feel trusting. I have complete freedom to talk to her. This is not a wasted trip.

We stop at the Kizyn house. Nadia needs a glass of water for her migraine, because she listened to her husband who talked on television until midnight; and he did not get home until 2 o'clock in the morning. It's an occasion to see the wells, whose big wheel she is turning, after opening the top. She brought the water back up like it was done in the country during my childhood. It must not be practical during the winter when it is freezing and snowing. Here, the buildings and life still follow the old country tradition that is starting to change by mechanization. Tractors are becoming more commonplace than horse-drawn vehicles. From the Kizyns, there is a long view of the chapel, 200 meters away. That's Maria's vantage point where she saw the silhouette for the first time. She is still seeing something. Nadia sees it too. She tells me, but I have a hard time understanding. It would be a black silhouette above the balcony located to the left of the chapel. I have always been baffled by this *"balcony"* talked about in English reports, and wonder if it has not a particular meaning, since a small chapel does not generally need a balcony. Through perseverance, Nadia makes me see, to the left of the building, a small wooden balcony. Yes, it really is a balcony, a whimsy of the builders, tiny, hardly visible from that distance. Above the balcony, she sees a black spot that would be the Blessed Virgin's silhouette.

It is as hard for me to see as to understand. I hardly see the tiny balcony, even less the tiny silhouette, a small black spot that could be, after all, an optical illusion. I am a good seer.

But all of this makes me understand how so many people saw and prayed to the Blessed Virgin on this balcony, when the chapel was closed, when one could only make out the inside through a keyhole. Did Maria Kizyn really see something more than the others? How did Josyp Terelya have six apparitions here similar to the one that saved his life, when he was dying of cold in his unheated Siberian prison? He does not speak of a balcony, or a cupola, where others saw a silhouette.

I go down to the doorway of the chapel. About twenty people are assembled. News circulates well in this village. But the farm woman has a hard time opening the three locks, and one of the keys does not work. It is our driver who overcomes the difficulty. After visiting the very modest small chapel and investigating the balcony where nothing is seen,

The inside of the Chapel in Gruchiv, built around a well whose clear water has long been famous for its miraculous power.

Maria Kizyn, the young prophet, whose modest visions sparked the great movement of pilgrimage and collective apparitions, at a key-time of the early liberalizations under perestroika

Maria Kizny, at the foot of the famous balcony from which she saw, from far away, the silhouette of the Grieving Virgin Mary.

I am dazzled by the splendor inside: a jewel of Ukrainian Baroque, hidden under a modest exterior.

The iconostasis is gleaming with gold and icons. They make me enter, inside, as priest. I find the same style of icons, sculptures, gildings, and a big missal with a clasp illuminated on the altar. There is not a speck of dust. This place is much visited with love. Here people pray with fervor.

At the center of the chapel, there is a well of pure water. The water is brought back by a short pulley.

On the wall, an icon represents the miraculous history of this well, tied, I do not know how, to the uprooting of a tree. I stand up on the small tribune, to see the balcony from inside. Popular piety had decorated it with beautiful elaborate cushions. Here the house of God is not a futile word. It is also the house of the Blessed Virgin.

125

There are a few chairs, and I can ask my questions of Maria, thanks to my friendly interpreter. The village is there, participating and intervening.

I first learn that the name really is Maria (and not Marina, as I had corrected, from the majority of the testimonies). Here are the notes of questions and her answers.

R.L. - How did it start?

Maria Kyzin - On April 26, 1987, at 9 o'clock in the morning, I was leaving for mass with a friend. It was Sunday. Mass was celebrated in another village. I saw, above the balcony of the chapel, the silhouette of the Blessed Virgin pacing back and forth.

R.L. - Were you afraid?

M.K - No.

R.L. - Surprised?

M.K. - Very much. And I went to tell my mother right away: "A woman is walking on the balcony" (pacing). My mother saw her too. My uncle and my aunt went to see below, by the chapel, but did not see anything on the balcony.

R.L. - And after that, did you see her often, at the same time?

M.K. - Almost every day, at the same time.

R.L. - But when did these apparitions stop?

M.K. - They are not over. I still see them.

R.L. - And you see clearly?

M.K. - Yes.

R.l. - Try to describe them.

M.K. - A black piece of clothing. One day, she had a white scarf which she waved.

R.L. - But the color of her eyes?

M.K. - I did not see. It was like a black and white photograph.

At that time people intervene:

A man - The police covered the balcony with a white tarp. But on that tarp, people saw the Blessed Virgin's icon.

R.L. - In color?

- No, black and white.

I go back to Maria:

R.L. - What was the message?

M.K. - No message?

R.L. - She did not speak to you?

M.K. - No.

At that time people intervene again, they are full of tales:

- One evening, the chapel was closed (watched by the police) and the door at the far end opened by itself.

If I understand right, Maria, who answers calmly and without overemphasizing anything, without a shadow of exaltation, only saw a very simple sign, very subtle. If she recognized the Blessed Virgin, it is not by her words. It is according to the tradition of this chapel, honored by ancient apparitions, and by an inner intuition or motion that comes to her. She is without shame or ostentation.

I search for the consequences of the apparitions. They have been considerable in the crowd that rediscovered the Blessed Virgin and prayer at a time when the stranglehold of atheism was beginning to relax.

R.L. - Are you more happy than you were before?

M.K. - I am better tempered. I am more religious. I go to mass every Sunday.

R.L. - Before, you did not go?

M.K. - I did, but not as regularly.

R.L. - Do you pray better since?

M.K. - Yes.

R.L - What do you prefer: apparitions or communion?

M.K. - Communion!

Good answer.

R.L. - Were you bothered by the police?

M.K. - For a while, they forced us to live in another village - Bruhovychy (70 kilometers away from there).

I then understand why so many witnesses had neither questioned nor saw her.

Afterwards, people participate.

R.L. - Why, after the big crowds of April-May 1987, are there so few people now?

-Every day, people come, hundreds on Sunday, and thousands for the three big celebrations of the Blessed Virgin.

R.L. - And when was this chapel returned to the Catholics?

- It belonged to the Orthodoxy as all Catholic chapels did, but it was strictly closed, since 1959. It was at Christmas 1989 that it was reopened, as a Catholic chapel.

For one year now, it has been remodeled with much love and taste.

What to conclude? The phenomenon is thin; a sign (should I say apparition?) without a message. The young Maria (born on June 20, 1976) saw, one morning, a black silhouette on the balcony of the chapel. That news was perceived as a signal. People came in large crowds from the Baltic countries and Georgia. Many followed them from everywhere. The formidable spiritual appetite of this people, forced into atheism, was watching for the Blessed Virgin, outlawed in this country, and found her presence again in prayer, or according to diverse forces of vision - most without any messages; others with messages, like Terelya.

His testimony, impressive but imprecise, had accentuated my positive conviction. But finally I came back, more precisely, to the diagnostic of my early edition (December 1988): an uncertain phenomenon, where no miracle is proven (although people speak of healings). But the subtle sign

Our Lady's message to Gruchiv

This is one of the extant version. She clarifies, by giving a mission to the Ukraine, the message of the conversion of Russia told by Our Lady to Fatima (1917) and Medjugorje.

"Teach your children to pray. Teach your children to live in truth and live your own life in truth. Forgive the nations that hurt you. Do not forget those who died in the Chernobyl disaster. Chernobyl is a reminder and a sign for the entire world. Say the Rosary constantly. The Rosary is the weapon against Satan. Satan fears the Rosary. Say the Rosary every day, constantly, in any gathering of people.

"I came deliberately to thank the Ukrainian people because you have suffered much for the Church of Christ for the last 70 years. I came to comfort you and tell you that your sufferings will soon end. The Ukraine will soon be an independent state.

"Convert yourselves and love each other. The times are coming, those which were predicted to be the last times. See the desolation surrounding the world: sins, laziness, genocide. I come with tears in my eyes; and I implore you, pray and work for goodness, for the glory of God. The Ukraine was the first country to recognize me as Queen, and I took her under my protection. Work for God because without it there is no possible happiness, and nobody will reach the Kingdom of God.

"You will win my heart and live in unity. Follow the Church leaders with audacity, and your country will be given back to you as well as power and love among the nations of the earth. I love the Ukraine and the Ukrainian people, for its sufferings and its fidelity to the Christ-King, and I will protect the Ukraine for the glory and the future of the Kingdom of God on earth. "Ukrainians must become Christ's Apostles among the Russian people, because if there is no return to Christianity in Russia, there will be a third world war."

served as a catalyst for an immense movement of fervor that played a considerable role at a key time when atheism was relaxing its asphyxiating chokehold. In the first edition of my book, I wrote:

"Do not smile and do not cry out to illuminism in the face of this drama of fear and faith. In Grouchevo, the Catholic Church is outlawed and underground. The asphyxiated faith feeds on the smallest signs and keeps the smallest icon as if it were a treasure. She is fertile in prophetic rumors [...]. The variety of rumors that have circulated on the subject of Grouchevo makes one think about the false rumors that circulated in Lourdes during the months when the Cave of Massabielle was forbidden But what does speak here is not exaltation, it is the permanent challenge of a faith in a state of acuteness, that knows how to find God in the emptiness into which it is thrown, by feeding on the smallest scraps."

I was citing here the testimonies of true believers, rigorous and critical, who had seen nothing extraordinary, but came back full of Our Lady and hope.

That's what I understood more concretely, more simply, with this young simple girl Maria. She does not have big projects for the future. She wants to marry, but wants to stay in this village, where she is growing up well. She and those farmers I met are a beautiful testimony, not only of a simple life, but of those middle classes of sanctity that comprise the Church. I did not find among them any trace of exaltation, but a trust and deep union to Our Lady, to God himself. Everything is under the sign of openness. That a phenomenon of authentic communication in prayer would not be sanctioned by a miracle or extraordinary fact that could be the object of a scientific report is really secondary in the eyes of faith. The important thing is that this communication exists, that it be alive. Happy are those who do not experience their Christianity as prisoners in this world, but discern, through the thick walls of our materialism, the small signs of God's love, which exist without being proved. They make for the happiness and the fecundity of our lives. This conclusion seems to have a general significance. "Faith does not stop at signs," Thomas Aquinas said, "but through them she reaches Reality."

Gruchiv, Chernobyl and the Apocalypse

The apparition in Gruchiv occurred on the morning of April 28. 1987, exactly a year after the catastrophe at the nuclear plant in Chernobyl, located about 500 kilometers from Gruchiv.

In Russian, Chernobyl means *absynthe* (a venomous plant). Ukrainains see in that fact the realization of the prophecy from the Apocalypse 8:11:

"The third angel played the trumpet, and from the heavens fell a large star burning like a torch. It fell on a third of the rivers and on the source of the waters. The name of the star is Absynthe (Russian: Chernobyl) and a third of the waters transformed into absynthe. Many men died of these waters because they had become bitter.

The analogy is striking: the atomic torch burns, it infects the earth and the waters. And that is how it caused many deaths.

BOOK IV

ROMANIA

1

In Bucarest

*Father Cosmovici at the time of my interview
with him in Bucharest, in November 1990*

HORIA COSMOVICI

Married priest, confessor of the Catholic faith

*Horia Cosmovici, octogenarian priest (born in 1909)
receives me in his small apartment in Bucarest with his wife
(the Romanian Greek-Catholic Church ordains married
priests, according to an ancient tradition that goes back to
Saint Paul). According to custom, he wears the black dress
and the Roman collar. At 81, he still preaches every week and
prolongs the immense influence he has exercised during his
hard captivity, up to his release in 1964. His health has
suffered from prison, but his mind is vigorous and lucid. His
house is filled a with icons.*

R. Laurentin - Horia Cosmovici, you have been a high
profile political man, Undersecretary of State at the Council

Presidence, with minister rank in 1940.

Horia Cosmovici - It was in 1943, under the influence of Mgr. Ghika that I went from Orthodoxy to Catholicism. At the time of my first contact with him, I had reacted negatively. I had sworn never to set foot in his house again, but I fell "victim" to his prayer. The second day I came back; the third day, he catechized me with the help of a small volume from J. Deharbes, and Ziliara for philosophy. It was useful to me, since I am a Doctor in Roman law. He sent a report to the Vatican to explain the steps I was taking. But the most profound reason for my conversion was not in his report. In fact, I was ambitious, wilful, sensual, and stubborn. It was my nature. I had to subdue him. It was to overcome this ambition that I converted, to become a Saint. In Orthodoxy, most certainly, one can become sanctified, but not a Saint, I believe, the Devil's assaults being what they are. Mgr. Ghika's last message was transmitted to me by another prisoner who had met him in his prison: "Tell my spiritual son Horia that I have prayed for him constantly and that at the time of death I give him my benediction." He died in 1946, two years before I received his message from the other world.

R.L. - How long were you in prison?

H.C. - 16 years, from 1948 to 1984; I had been in limited internment as early as 1944. In 1948, a new sentence gave me 10 years... and it was extended. I was sent to work in the Danube delta, cutting reeds. You cut your hands at it. If somebody died, he was thrown in the river, without any more ado. I was arrested for pleading a case the government did not like, I was a lawyer.

R.L. - What was the work pace?

H.C. - Every day, even Sunday, the whole day, from sunrise to sunset; in summer, the wakeup call was at 4 in the morning. Work started at 5, and lasted to the evening.

R.L. - What is the use of these reeds?

H.C. - We made paper out of them.

R.L. - Among those who were in forced labor camps, were they many Christians?

H.C. - Mostly Christians, Catholic and Orthodox; we, the Catholics, were more active. I saw a secret Mass in the attics we lived in. We took advantage of a time when the guard, tired, was asleep. We were lying on straw, head in hands, elbows on the ground, to hide what we were doing. He did not wake up before the end.

R.L. - Your state of health?

H.C. - My weight was only 44 kilos.

R.L. - Instead of how much now?

H.C. - 70! My skin had lost its flexibility. I had scabs.

R.L. - But was there not an infirmary, sick time?

H.C. - An infirmary, but hardly any sick time. The scabs were not a sufficient reason!

R.L. - In these deplorable conditions, what were you able to do?

H.C. - Catechetics. I elaborated on them in my head. The prisoners were thirsty for there teachings it. The Catechetics would form during the night, after I was working. I transmitted there thoughts as they occurred.

R.L. - Did these Catechetics reflect your experience with God?

H.C. - One of my companions, Nicolas, who had been in only two grade school classes, a lumberjack in Transylvania and Greek-Catholic, meditated on the Rosary according to the method I taught him. He spent the whole morning on one Mystery. He told me his impressions: "Ah, poor God! That he forgives me for speaking of him in such a way; when I think that He fell on the Way of the Cross! If He could have gone one step further, surely He would have done it. And me, I am a sinner!" I told Nicolas: "When you meditate on the Mysteries, do not linger on the taking away of the clothes, that horror!" -"No," he said, "because He is above shame!" He is the most profound man I ever met. He had three children. Maybe he is still alive.

R.L. - What was this method of praying that affected your companion in such a way?

H.C. - Nothing extraordinary. I began thinking about it in the night I did not sleep on my cot, but I was not even tired. It appeared to me that there was a hiatus between the Joyful Mysteries which end when Jesus was 12, and the Sorrowful Mysteries that begin with the Passion when he was 33. Between the two, there was His entire hidden life, His entire public life. This is how the *social Rosary* was formed in me. I added 5 other mysteries. My intuition is part of the family. It was formed for the family. It is the essential to the order I founded. One says, "Everything changes", but why is the change we see regrettable? Because we have polluted life. We took women. We threw them into the work force. We left children in the street, chatting. Let's give women a salary and allow them to stay at home so that the family lives. It is with this perspective that I clearly saw the Rosary during my nights.

R.L. - What were the mysteries of your third and the next to the last series?

H.C. - Five mysteries: 1. The hidden life; 2. The baptism ending the prophecies; 3. The wedding of Cana, the first miracle performed for a wedding; 4. The public life; and 5. The Last Supper- the Eucharist.

R.L. - You have built upon this prayer the Order of the Rose. When did you get this idea?

H.C. - As early as 1948, I then asked for an sign. A parish priest was in the next cell. He had heart disease, that gave him the right to half a liter of milk a day. He would give me half of it when the guard was relieved. On the day I asked for my sign, I went to get my milk, as usual, at the best time... hurriedly, because of the short time available. But that priest made me sit down: "Listen," he said, "I had a dream. I was in Rome; I was bringing lots of flowers and suddenly they all wilted, except for a rose, sheltered by the wall of the Church." Nothing else, but I had my sign. The rose will not wilt.

R.L. - Family occupies a great place in your intuition. Can you tell me some of the main ideas?

H.C. - (He looks through his small typed volume, the Order of the Rose). I insist on articulating well (Christian) instruction and education. Each child is a world unto himself, a universe apart, the unique solution. The great problem with education is to find this solution "good for one time only". To this end, the biological element is decisive and inescapable. What the best educator will do with lots of difficult and mediocre cases, the father and especially the mother will do on equal footing and easily because they carry this unique solution in their blood, in their instincts. That is why, at the foundation of Christian politics, there are two institutions -

the Church (with its particular way of teaching) and the Christian family.

R.L. - I believe that is the conclusion in your little book.

H.C. - Yes, and I finish that last political chapter that way: "God's seal is sacrament. Socially, God only reserved two sacraments: marriage and the Order - marriage that gives birth to Christians in the world, and the Order that lowers Christ from the Altar.

R.L. - It is your grace to have been able to assure both, as a married priest in the Greek-Catholic Church... But how did your release occur?

H.C. - In 1964, President Johnson decided on an important aid to Romania. One of his friend told him: "Do not give this aid without first assuring release of political prisoners."

R.L. - How are your marriage and ordination related to one another in time?

H.C. - I was married in 1944. My first arrest happened 10 days later, after a visit from the police and a search. I was ordained a priest in 1965, a year after my release.

R.L. - Did you continue to exercise a profession?

H.C. - I tried to regain my profession as a lawyer, but I really could not anymore. There was no more justice. I changed my situation to economist. It was proposed to me to become an ordained priest, because my Catholic faith was known. Bishop Luliu Hirtea, a Greek-Catholic, asked me: "Do you want to become a priest?" - "I do not know theology," I objected. "I read your book, Manual for the Christian Political Man."

R.L. - Was it a book you published before your imprisonment?

H.C. - No.

R.L. - A manuscript then?

H.C. - No. I had dictated that text to one of my companions in captivity. He wrote it on the prison wall with a needle, and began to learn it. But he changed cells. So I gave him the text again, in Morse code, on our common wall, long = 2; short = 1 (he mimes the striking on the table in an alert rhythm) When we were finished, he knew the text by heart, and me too. We repeated it like a catechism. We shared it.

R.L. - Then it was a short text?

H.C. - Yes, condensed. Once free, I wrote it, 71 pages. Here it is.

R.L. - It's in French!

H.C. - Yes, I would say it in French, because, with our guards, it was okay. French lessons were respected. Under this cover, we would say what was important to say.

R.L. - That text was kind of a chart of the Order of the Rose?

H.C. - Yes.

R.L. - How many members? Was it a large movement?

H.C. - No, the Order was limited to 10 members (not including myself). Two died. I did not replace them. I did not want to enlarge the Order itself. But many others live with that message, that is at the same time catechetics and a program. It is not and does not seek to be an organization, a little bit like the priests of Dom Gobbi. Our group of 10 and I get together only twice a year.

R.L. - But how did Mgr. Luliu Hirtea know of this text as early as 1965?

H.C. - It is because in 1952 I was released for 100 days (like Napoleon!). The first thing I did was to write the text that I had learned by heart, so I would not forget it.

R.L. - What was your activity as a priest?

H.C. - Preaching.

R.L. - You probably also celebrated mass?

H.C. - Not publicly.

R.L. - Why?

H.C. - It's because I lost an eye, in 1953, while cutting reeds.

R.L. - A work accident?

H.C. - Yes. It was November 21, 1953. The basic model chainsaw sent off pieces of wood. One eye had to be taken out.

R.L. - Right away? An emergency?

H.C. - No, 4 or 5 months later, and without anesthesia. I then had one eye missing and I have cataracts in the other one. I do not feel like celebrating publicly. That is why I settle for preaching in the parish. I do catechetics and I founded the Institute Vladimir Ghika with Mister Ayed of Paris.

The meeting is over, I ask Horis for his benediction. He takes me to the chapel. He takes his Greek-Catholic stole, large white band that falls on the front and back, with a V-cut around the neck. We pray together. God's life shines in this man. With simple texts and a new meditation of the Rosary, he deeply affected a whole generation, filled with the experience of God.

2

In Cluj

Tertullien Lango, general curate of the parish and grand-father, with his grand-children. The son of a university professor, a priest ordained in secret

Vicar-General TERTULLIEN LANGA

Heroic history of a family of priests

Father Tertullien Langa illustrates well the heroism of the Romanian Greek-Catholic Church, categorized Uniat. Abolished by Communism, given away to the more docile Orthodoxy, it has survived for 40 years in the catacombs. Of the 6 Bishops of that Church, all imprisoned in 1948, and of the 5 others ordained in secret after that, 9 died from the torments to which they were subjected.

At the beginning of this drama, Tertullien Langa, born on October 26, 1922, was a young married college student; was expecting the birth of his first daughter. How did he become an underground priest, him, then his brother-in law, while waiting the ordination of his son who is preparing himself for becoming a non-married priest?

Actually, Tertullien is Vicar-General of the Diocese of Cluj (a university town, the Romanians' Tubingen), and would probably be bishop if that function was not reserved for non-married priests.

"He was offered the Episcopate," a Romanian Christian told me, "because he is the strong man of our Church; but he did not want to impose on his wife another separation (another infidelity), after the one from so many years in prison."

Here I am in front of him, at the "Archbishop's Palace of Cluj". That panel was just put back on the door, but the Palace is still seized. The government has promised to give it back, as well as other Greek-Catholic buildings, through a decree that is still in abeyance. It is only from the kindness of the director of the School for the Handicapped, *located in the old Archbishop's Palace, that two rooms were symbolically conceded. We must concentrate on these ridiculous premises all of the activity of a diocese without churches, deprived of its means of existence. Greek-Catholics always were reduced to celebrate mass outside, in summer as in winter, in the sun as well as in the rain.*

Tertullien Langa's height, powerful frame, and vigorous and clear logic were impressive, but these will not hide for very long the heart and passion that secretly inhabit him. He tells me of his program, fights and difficulties. I insist on discovering this grandfather's secret, patriarch of a beautiful family, who wears rigorously the Roman collar of Vicar-General.

R. Laurentin - What I mostly want to know about is your underground activity. When did it begin?

Tertullien Langa - In prison. I had just gotten married. My wife was 3 month pregnant. I was 23. During the war I had started college studies in Philosophy, Law and Theology, first in Blaj, center of the Greek-Catholic Metropole, with Tite Live Kinesu, rector of the Faculty of Theology, then, in Bucharest, with Mgr. Vladimir Ghika (a great figure of the Romanian Church whose canonization cause is open). He had come back from abroad "to share the sufferings of his people". My director of conscience was Bishop, soon to be martyr, Mgr. Suciu. I was an assistant to the University Chair of Theology of Bucharest, as well as Pedagogy.

R.L. - Why were you imprisoned?

T.L. - For helping people in trouble. But it probably was a pretext. The activity for which you question me began in prison.

R.L. - Was the prison hard?

He lays the question aside with a gesture, and only answers:

T.L. - This period of my life was the most productive and the happiest of all my personal and missionary life. Look! If in that prison I had the occasion to introduce God to just one soul, then those years won an eternity. In terms of so many eternities thus won, what I had to endure was superfluous.

R.L. - But your prison?

T.L. - No use talking about it.

R.L. - Christ's passion was also a horror - no use talking about it. However, the four Evangelists describe it. Christ's Passion, continued in our Church is not different.

T.L. - Since you insist, here is one aspect. During the first three months, it was impossible to sleep. It was winter. I was in an empty room without a mattress, blanket or furniture. I only had a pair of pants, a short-sleeved shirt and 700 calories a day in food.

R.L. - Black bread?

T.L. - No, some corn. And they had taken the window off.

R.L. - The window, but not the bars?

T.L. - Of course! In that cold, I could not sleep.

R.L. - You were at risk of freezing to death?

T.L. - Yes, that's why you could survive only if you walked day and night, back and forth, in that small 3 by 2 meter room. From 11:30 to noon, the sun came in. For this half an hour, with the sun on me, I slept crouching down.

R.L. - Crouching down? Why not lying down?

T.L. - The ground was too cold. In the next room was Petru Tomescu, ex-Minister of Public Health. It was he who strongly advised me not to ever sleep, because he "who sleeps does not wake up".

R.L. - Then, many died?

T.L. - Out of 60 at the beginning of winter, 28 were left in the spring. Since you want significant episodes, here is one. On the other side of my room was Admiral Macellaru. One evening, I was surprised not to hear him walk next door. I listened carefully. I heard his voice: "I am going to tell you about a dream." - "Did you sleep?" - "Yes, I had a wonderful dream: the moon in a huge sky, like a corn polenta. I kneeled down and I prayed God to make that moon fall in my room. God answered my prayer and, with the moon in my room, I laid down on the floor and I ate my fill. Now excuse me, I want to continue my dream." Two hours later (at 6 o'clock in the morning), when the guard opened the door, he found a body. He was dead, the famous Admiral, dreaming he was eating the moon.

Visit to the unknown father

Other witnesses told me of other sufferings during that captivity. The torture of loneliness alternated with the one of crowding. There were so many prisoners in the cell that you could not lie down or sit. They had organized turns, so that some could crouch down and sleep while the others kept close.

Tertullien's daughter, Marie Emmanuelle, born 6 months after his incarceration, told me about another detail that Tertullien's modesty had hidden from me. She did not know him, but her mother had raised her in the cult of her father. Emmanuelle knew of his heroism.

Marie Emmanuelle in 1956 fortuitously, a unique permission was granted to the prisoners' families to see them. That is when I discovered this unknown father.

R.L. - Were you able to kiss him?

Marie Emmanuelle - Wait! There was a small wall between us. Behind that small wall, barbed wire, then another small wall, and in the second corridor, between that wall and my father, the guard. But I wanted so much to see him more closely that I slipped through the barbed wire, asking the guard permission to approach him. My father kissed me between the barbed wire. That kiss was fiery. It was a great joy that vanquished my pain. The visit lasted 10 minutes. My mother and he exchanged few words, but I felt a profound communication through their laconism. I did not see him again after that, for 9 years, until I was 16.

Now I am returning to the interview with Tertullien Langa.

R.L. - How is it that you were in prison with an admiral and an ex-minister?

T.L. - I was only 26. I don't know why, but I had been put among the dangerous enemies of Antonescu. I was not dangerous. But Providence wanted this chance among others. I still cannot understand it all today. But I learned a little bit at a time that everything has a purpose. I am grateful to God and also to those who were the hard instrument of Providence.

R.L. - You mean your tormentors?

A subtle inclination of the head tells me I understood. Tertullien has a practical and realistic style, but he constantly refers everything to God.

It is only in 1964, after 16 years in prison, that he saw his wife and his 16-year-old daughter again, and, there again, it is to them I had to turn to know what his modesty and meditative words do not spell out.

Marie Emmanuelle - When I saw him again, 9 years after my visit to the prison, my parents kissed each other without saying anything. Their understanding of each other was beyond words. It was a grace from God, given to my mother, to make me understand this absent father. He was not a stranger to me. I had understood his heroism in full truth. I was very proud, in spite of my fear. Everything happened discretely. My father has become my best friend.

Marie Emmanuelle learned of his priestly ordination afterwards. Since it was secret, she believes he was ordained in captivity when he had only been approached. In fact it was after, and it is he we must now hear on this point.

Secret ordination

Tertullien Langa - Immediately after my liberation from prison, in 1964, three bishops made contact with me and offered that I be ordained in secret. I accepted, and I received the priestly ordination in October. I have noticed that God did answer my prayer (here, a subtle smile).

R.L. - What do you mean?

T.L. - During the captivity, I asked him to celebrate at least *one single mass* in my life. He has granted me more than a thousand.

R.L. - Then more than a hundredfold! Where was your first mass celebrated?

T.L. - It was in Cluj where my wife and daughter lived. I had addressed another prayer to God. If you want to liberate me from this prison, let me have a son for a priest. Once again, he did not listen to me. He did not give me one son but two - my own son, who is going to a seminary in Rome soon to be ordained a non-married priest, and the university professor my daughter married who was a secretly ordained priest.

I met the young university professor, Anton Gotia, married in 1972, a priest since 1974. I will introduce him later.

I asked vicar-general Tertullien Langa,

R.L. - What was your life like when you returned?

152

T.L. - When I left the prison, I was unemployed at first. Then I was a laborer, then a doorman at a college. At that time, I could not aim higher, because all my papers and diplomas had been confiscated at the time of my arrest. I could not give any proof of my credentials. By being patient, I was able to find a copy of my General Certificate of Education, then my Bachelor of Arts in Philosophy; but nobody dared hire me... as an outlaw. A research institute looking for a translator hired me, at the salary of a semi-skilled worker. I translated Italian, English, and French. After a few months, I took a competitive examination in Industrial Psychology. I passed the test and obtained an intellectual professional status. It was very useful for taking care of my family. I worked that way until retirement at age 60, in 1983.

During that time of professional activity, I was a researcher in the morning and a priest in the afternoon. I gave lessons in catechism, putting 2 to 5 children, mostly students, in groups. Later, with more audacity, and under divine protection, I met with groups of about ten young people every week in Judge Vasile Farcas' generous house. This house was the only church and cathedral of Cluj! There, spiritual education was given to hundreds of young people, with one of the spiritual masters of that generation, Father Mattei Boila.

This priest attended the interview. I later questioned him also.

T.L. - Other houses harbored my meetings, the houses of the painter and of Mrs. Miltran, M.D.

400 vocations without a seminary

R.L. - How did you avoid going back to prison?

T.L. - In fact, *Securitate* knew. Judge Vasile Farcas, myself, and others were often threatened by officers, but with

153

the help of the Holy Spirit we were able to go on. We were not the only ones; many others did the same thing. Dozens, hundreds of young people took a direction towards theology. It was in that climate that I came out of the underground last December. Vocations were numerous. More than 400 candidates. Everything was and remains confiscated. We can say mass outside, but we cannot train priests. A place is necessary.

R.L. - Then what do you do?

T.L. - We began here, with about forty seminarists. The School for the Impaired, which was established in the old archbishop's place by the State, closes at 4 o'clock in the afternoon. They let me use a room to teach Theology. Forty come, as many as the room can take.

I looked at that room, 7 by 8 meters, full of large tables close together. In the evening, I met the 40 seminarists. They all have another job in order to survive. Those I questioned ranged from 23 to 47 years of age. One has been a steel worker since age 15; another is a professor; another, a finisher in paper manufacturing; another, a student, gave up his studies to give himself completely to Theology; another is a principal in a high-school; another, a technician; another, a biologist (licensed). Most of them are married. They did not hesitate to hold these studies along with a profession and a family life, they are calm and strong people.

It will be said, how good that the clergy can be married! Yes, this change was vital in saving the Greek-Catholic Church, but latitudinarian conclusions should not be drawn. Their concept of married clergy is founded on heroism and forges ahead. Those who would base its foundation on convenience, without the support of a living tradition and a profound conviction, would end in disaster. While in the West you so often meet priests and may wonder if they really are priests. These "fathers" both in the human and supernatural sense, radiate the image of God. Their priesthood permeates their personal and family lives. I felt this intensely when in contact with these realistic and devoted people.

A call

Tertullien Langa did not give any more details. He wanted to conclude.

T.L. - Up until last year we held meetings in the woods and cemeteries. After the "liberation", we still had to celebrate mass outside. But finally, we were free! All know well that it is the result of the sacrifice accepted by the bishops from the bottom of their hearts, who gave their lives to save their ties with the Holy See. None of them gave up. They died for it. The sacrifice founded the spiritual stature of our Church. It is still missing a physical location necessary to its activity. All our possessions are confiscated. The Romanian State, which has planned the restitution, flounders in its endless evasiveness; and the Orthodox are fiercely opposed to the restitution of our churches.

I wrote and talked about it in with President Iliescu: "Liberty without a necessary physical place has no meaning. It is not liberty. Today, we have gained the freedom to practice our cult, but in the open air."

If God has caused so many vocations in our Church, we can be convinced that these vocations have the right to a necessary physical place for cultivation and the required actions for the salvation of the soul.

I added that on the inside level, we resorted to all means available to solve the outside level of our Church, but with no result. Today (November 23, 1990) there is no hope from the

Romanian State or from the Orthodoxy. However, we still keep hope, on the natural and supernatural levels.

On the natural level, the only means of influencing the politics at home is the fear that the abuses will compromise the economic and political aid from foreign countries. It would be desirable to have the Western Countries require the respect of human rights for that aid. That is how I was liberated in 1964, the United Staes only gave its aid, then considerable and very necessary, at the price of the liberation of political prisoners. That was done, that is how I was freed.

On the supernatural level. It is impossible that Providence would turn a deaf ear to such a great capital of prayer, suffering, and deeds (There are about ten bishops, hundreds of priests, and thousands of seculars). God is always with us; we keep an unshakable trust. We remain grateful to the Holy Spirit which gives us the understanding of events, and makes us know so clearly, in this incredible slalom, the way of God who remains with us.

3

ANTON GOTIA

University professor, priest, father of five children

It is Anton Gotia, Tertullien Langa's Son-in-law, who greeted me, with a car at the airport. I concentrate here on our conversations which occurred on several occasions, including in his home, with his beautiful family of five children and with his wife, Marie Emmanuelle, Tertullien Langa's daughter.

Anton Gotia - I did my college studies from 1963 to 1968 and then a lecturer position in Budapest, between 1969 and 1973, as part of the Romanian-Hungarian exchange program. In 1958, I was elected to the Faculty of Arts in Cluj - language, and history of the Romanian language, and studies of ancient texts.

In answer to my questions on the Romanian language, Anton Gotia answered,

It is a language of Latin origin, with some Slavic elements. Romanian is the first pillar of Romanity, with French, Spanish and Italian the sole survivors of eastern Latinhood. It is important, notably for identifying the words of Latin origin in Italian. Our language alphabet was Cyrillic up to the XIXth century. But the School of Transylvania fought for the introduction of the Latin alphabet.

It was in 1972 that I married Marie Emmanuelle Langa and it was in 1974 that I was ordained a priest. In spite of our five children, my wife must keep working (she teaches languages), because salaries are low and prices go up, only 20% for food. For everything else, 130%.

R.L. - How did your ordination happen?

A.G. - A priest, a friend of Father Langa, asked me, "Have you ever thought about becoming a priest?" - "No, I am trying to lead a spiritual life." A bishop who was in contact with me insisted. In normal times, the education requires a long time. But in exceptional times and urgency, it is faster. My vocation comes from an appeal from the Church. I heard it and answered right away. I pursued the necessary studies: dogmatic, ascetic, mystical, sacraments, morals, and confession. I first received the minor orders, and I was ordained deacon and priest in secrecy. I practiced discreetly a cult of the catacombs, in contact with the Ordinary of the Diocese who had not been able to be ordained bishop and was employed at the student's Polyclinic. He became my spiritual guide, a good guide. It is Hirtes Chirtea who ordained me in secret. He is dead. Tertullien Langa was present at the ordination.

R.L. - And your wife? *I asked.*

A.G. - No, she was expecting our second child.

R.L. - What were your activities?

A.G. - They were discreet, without publicity. We met groups with young people who did not know I was a priest, but the group was clandestine. We met regularly several times a month for catechism, prayer, meditation, sharing of experience, and charitable action. We were known as the *Focolari* movement.

During the last few years, police surveillance has relaxed. It was dangerous, and we were always on the look out. It formed people who were committed, active, and devoted to the Church.

At the University, I had given lectures on the genesis of the Romanian people. I studied and taught Protochristianity... as part of the official program.

During the last years, I talked more explicitly of the Church on a historical ground. It was very new, very accepted. An Orthodox book had been published on Protochristianity. It gave me a reference. This year, I have been able to have a course in Christian history and spirituality.

For mass, caution was required. I celebrated mass in small circles, mostly in my family. I began publicly in February 1990. At Easter, during the underground period, the liturgy of the Resurrection was sung in an undertone.

R.L. - What are the fruits of this experience and this ministry?

A.G. - In my family, God has given us plentiful graces of understanding, unity, and patience through difficulties. It helped with education, and to get through health problems. It also gave us a balance, an inner joy.

In meetings, many people have found a spiritual life that fulfilled their wait and their hope. Vocations arose in young people with whom I met. They are now engaged in seminary courses that are conducted in the Archbishop's Palace. Many of them are married. For the young ones, I made contact with Mattei Boila. He probably did not know that I was a priest. It was not necessary, then, that all priests knew of each other. My father-in-law Tertullien Langa was the source of many vocations. When he was arrested in 1948, it was for "supporting disobedience". He had helped the wife of the director of the factory of Recita, whose factory had been confiscated. He was indicted for "help to infringement".[1]

4

MATTEI BOILA

Married priest, 4 children

Saturday, November 4, was my last day in Cluj. After meeting the Bishop there, in the Archbishop's Palace where a few coins were left for him, I took the bus which went up the hill for the burial of a theologian in his village, who had just died. We arrived early. I took the occasion to collect, in the mini-bus, the testimony of Father Mattei Boila, son-in-law of Judge Farcas, who put his authority in jeopardy by protecting outlawed Greek-Catholics.

-I was born on April 17, 1926. I was ordained a priest after getting out of prison, in 1965.

I was raised in the Greek-Catholic Church, but I took my distance, not because of philosophical and rational doubt, but because of objections or pretexts.

My most severe prison was the canal of the Danube. It was an extermination camp at the mouth of the river. My luck was that I was not left there for long because of a friend who was being investigated. I was transferred to a less destructive, but hard camp. There were 240 crammed together in 4 cells made for 8 prisoners. There were more than 50 of us in each cell. It was impossible to lie down to sleep.

In October 1953, the door opened. An old man with a white beard, without a jacket or a shirt, just underwear, was thrown among us. We then learned who he was Mgr. Vladimir Ghika.

We took a collection to free him. I had a good sweater my sister made. I gave it to him. At first he refused to take it, but as we insisted, he ended up accepting it. He recognized and blessed me. He knew my family. I told him everything:

"I do not belong to the Church, I do not believe."

"No, you believe; you do not know what I know."

He blessed me, and at that time I understood that I would not escape upon my return home. It was the end of exile. I spent a month with him; then I was liberated. He died in the prison of Villaba. He had predicted,

"I will die on Wednesday."

Among the prisoners, I saw a lot of courage, but only two were totally free. Prison did not exist for them - Ghika, and an Orthodox, Lovanni, a monk.

I had an administrative, not penal, sentence, a year in prison. After the death of Stalin, administrative sentences were eliminated. I converted on my return. Many prayed for me.

I then worked as a collier, for the boring of oil wells.

In 1955-1956, Romania joined the ONU. We wrote a memoir to manifest that Communism was arbitrary, dictatorial and without freedom. I was turned in and we were arrested. It was in 1956, a new prison, less hard, in Jibala, but we were hungry and cold. We were submitted to moral pressures and all sorts of troubles. I had the feeling I was at God's disposition. I was telling him: "I know my weakness, support me!" And God supported my humility.

I was in prison with Mgr Iuliu Hirta, archbishop, and Dragomir. Everyday Hirta said an homily. There were 242 of us in the four adjoining rooms, still in Jilaba. We were in retreat for the 42 days of Lent. He then was able to say mass discreetly with underground bread and wine. The 242, of all ages, professions, and levels of faith, received the Holy Communion.

Liberated in 1944, I got married to Judge Farcas' daughter, one of the great supporters of the Greek-Catholic Church. He has immense courage. I have four children. Two are in Paris.

Being a jurist, I teach Canon Law at the seminary, and I translated the new Canonic Code of Rights into Romanian.

RECENTLY I assisted at the ordination of two priests in the open air, since we do not have churches, and I preach the homily every week on Cluj-Radio. During those last few days, I felt I was acting, not by my power, but by the power of God, like Abraham, sterile and fecund. I am certain that the future of our Church is assured.

In the underground period, I celebrated mass everyday at Judge Farcas' home. I married his daughter so it was also my house. I trained young people on Sundays. Everything began from there. The *Securitate* (the police) still did not allow this, but did not arrest anymore. It was tolerated if we were discreet.

In those years, a priest was arrested.

"We will liberate you if you stop your liturgies," the policemen told him.

"Arrest me, because if I am free, I will go on."

They did not arrest him. Me, I was asked to guarantee that I would not celebrate anymore. I said,

"No way, you arrest me. I will defend myself in front of the judge and I will prove that it is you who are breaking the law."

It was a month before the revolution. They stopped and did not intervene.

On our return Mattei Boila took me to visit Judge Farcas' home in which he still lives. His house was one of the sanctuaries of the underground Church.

5

Mgr ALEXANDER TODA

Metropolite of the Greek-Catholics, in Blaj

While I was interviewing Mattei Boila in the mini-bus that took me from Cluj to the next hill, I received a prestigious visit: the number one figure in the Greek-Catholic Church, Metropolite Toda, 76 years old. Time was short, so I asked him to tell me, quickly, his curriculum:

-I was arrested in 1948. I escaped, and I was able to disappear for 2 years. That is when I was ordained a bishop, Latin Archbishop of Bucharest. I was caught, arrested seven times, and sentenced to life. I spent 26 years in prison, from 1948 to 1964. I was liberated on President Johnson's request. He had put as a condition to the American aid the liberation of political prisoners. In my metropolitan town, Blaj, the seminary is used as a hospital. We are trying to get a part of it back. The seminary receives married and single priests. The last ones must choose their life state before ordination.

The Metropolite is coming back from Paris, where he asked for Cardinal Lustiger's help.

6

Burial in the open air of theologian

GABRIEL POP, 89 years old,

in the hills of Cluj

During my trip, the theologian Gabriel Pop, the most well-known of the Romanian Greek-Catholic theologians, 89 years old, ex-student of Garrigou-Lagrange, died in Beleac, near Cluj.

Here like elsewhere, the Orthodox have received the Catholic Church from the government, and they are not willing to share or give it back. Thus it is in the open air, in the fields, near the edge of a thatched cottage, that the Ukrainian Metropolite comes to celebrate the burial. We are on a high hill, at the edge of a village with its thatched roofs. It is Metropolite Alexander Toda who celebrates.

According to the local customs, the coffin is open. The emaciated face of the old man emerges - long beard, an embroidered veil on his body, covered with sacerdotal ornaments, flowers on his feet.

The Metropolite celebrates the Eucharist, with his violet calotte, the solemnity of which contrasts with the wintery dreariness and the earthy ground. Two mortuary crowns of local fabrication are around the coffin. Those who come hold crosses and banners. The wind bothers the candles but does not put them out.

The catacombs continue, on the November crushed grass, lightened sometimes by a pale sun. Will the Greek-Catholics, called Uniates, be sacrificed until the end, before and after persecution that has no end for them?

7

PRISONS OF WOMEN

The testimony of Doctor GISCA VIORICA

She is the wife of a famous painter, recently deceased. It is she who gave me hospitality in Bucharest.

-I was also arrested, in 1949,. We were political prisoners in common law. We were more than 20 women in 40 square meters. No bathroom. A chamber pot in a corner. We went there by walking on the others. One day, there was dysentery. It was terrible.

We stayed like this for a month, without a blanket, in a humid cellar. We had humidity mushrooms on our faces. We were political prisoners. I was with Sister Constantina. We prayed, but not together. We indicated it by the sign of the cross. Sometimes, we would say

"Leave me alone, I am praying."

The worst was at the beginning. Towards the end I regained my cheerfulness.

"You are crazy, the others would tell me."

Inside I was gloomy. I was telling myself, "We will never survive". Mgr Ghika was praying for me. I woke up one morning as if a dark veil had lifted. I was perceiving the light. I thought, "Everything will be OK."

I was court-martialed after 10 months. I was sentenced for helping people in distress.

In prison, I meditated. We are not alone if we have God.

8

TOO MANY BISHOPS

The surplus of the underground and mysticism

Under Ceaucescu, I had been contacted by the community of Sister Ionella, a community with a charismatic style, then underground and threatened (I helped some members to obtain political asylum in France). It was a place of extraordinary events: ecstasies, apparitions (discreet) and the stigmata of Sister Ionella, bleeding hosts and crucifix (since 1949), etc. The Nuncio and Rome knew about it. The crucifix remained in the Nuncio's residence.

It would be premature to perceive, especially since this discreet and fervent community has discovered, with freedom, new unresolved difficulties.

This community has found itself tied to the underground Church and to the secret ordination of priests. The three bishops tied to this community, notably Bishop Justin, who came in with some other priests, are not recognized. The regular Greek-Catholic hierarchy, which came out of the underground, considers these ordinations to be unwarranted. However, they were done by Bishop Dragomir, who then was number one in the Greek Catholic Church, and the ordination documents are preserved. But the bishop would have overstepped his power of exception by ordaining three bishops instead of one. These bishops are thus challenged. They are asked to sign an unconditional resignation before any discussion.

On the other hand, Sister Ionella had belonged to a flourishing congregation that was opposed to her with a file of arguments in support. She was examined by a Jesuit, Father Raphael Haag, of German origin, in 1946-1948. He investigated, according to Saint Phillipe de Neri, by putting Sister Ionella to the test. He asked her to leave the community she founded. She thought she had to refuse, and consequently the judgment was negative. But Professor Aurel Leutiu held a favorable judgment, including that of the visions and extraordinary phenomenon.

The situation is thus tense. The community continues. It remains at the center of fervent prayer. The police threats, which had destroyed the house, have stopped, but the community is still marginal. Many come to pray with a fervor adversaries call illuministic. But where fervor is grand, where does illuminism begin?

This community, which heard of my trip to Romania, was waiting for me at the airport. I paid them a visit, and I heard all sides of their story, positive and negative.

Here again, Father Tertullien Langa gave me a good judgement, spiritual and critical, in which I recognized, as in other things, the measure of his perfect lucidity. "I refrain from a personal opinion," he said to me in substance. "The case is delicate and contested. Mystical phenomena are authentic for some, hysteria or illusion for others. As for me, I would have wished the case was authentic, from professional pride, and not from embarrassment, but in order to preserve my Church, if it came to that. Up until now there has not been a serious and scientific examination. It would be desirable."

What is certain is that Sister Ionella's Community has awakened profound and lasting fervor, and the ones I know are balanced, sincere, and patient. It would be desirable that the problem be solved, not by force, but, if possible, by conciliation and channeling of this generous movement. This would call for, with a new examination, a dialogue which would be difficult on both sides, tension having a tendency to lock each side in its own point of view. It may be that the Nuncio, arriving in Bucharest at the end of my short visit, may find a solution to this conflict. The relation between spontaneous *hierarchy* and *charisma* is usually difficult. It often becomes a dialogue of the deaf and a show of power. It requires openness and humility on both sides. If these are missing on either side, the tension becomes unsolvable; and the forces of the Church are wasted. It is in this domain that Satan achieves his masterpieces of division and confusion.

My short visit abroad did not allow me to judge such a complex affair. Most certainly, fervor is not absent from this inextricable adventure. The slogan "Let them live" is also applicable to God's blessings, even where favor must be refined, purified, and uprooted from the human and the over human.

It is not by chance that Tradition compares the Church to Noah's ark, in which different and enemy species, apparently born to devour each other lived in harmony. It is the vocation of the Church to achieve the concordance of differences: *concordantia discordantium*, according to the beautiful Latin formula.

Should we have said nothing about this painful affair? No, discretion or respect is not necessarily silence, and this conflict has the interest of manifesting an aspect of the underground that should not be idealized in all aspects. If it has caused wonderful initiatives, it also can implicate divergences and overabundance, unbearable at a time of ecclesiastical reorganizations: an overabundance of bishops, ordained under heroic conditions that are no longer in use, mystical overabundance which was a sign of hope in persecution but seems troubling or sectarian today.

And then, as in the war of 1914 (and all the wars), this was a time of heroism for the ardent and generous temperaments less adapted to ordinary life. This is like the times of persecuted Christian resistance during which exceptional Christians show their mettle but find themselves unwanted when ordinary life is reestablished.

BOOK V

POLAND

1

*The victorious Church in a time
of tensions and responsibilities*

Cardinal JOSEPH GLEMP

Primate of Poland

*I met Cardinal Glemp in Csestochowa, where he presided
over the closing of the Congress on the Virgin Mary (September 20-23, 1990). He received me in the apartments reserved
for the Primate in the national sanctuary: a beautiful building with antique furniture and paintings that take you to
another world, full of memories. Czestochowa is the holy
place in Poland. It is there that Cardinal Wyszynski (Glemp's
predecessor) sent from his prison, on August 26, 1956, the
consecration that was the signal of liberation and the starting
point of all Polish victories.*

R. Laurentin - Mister Cardinal, how do you see
POLAND"S FUTURE?

Cardinal J. Glemp - We are at a turning point. Jaruzelski
is leaving. The people will choose his future democratically.
I hope that God will help, as in the past.

R.L. - This turning point is also a grave economic crisis,
that come from afar: inflation increases faster than the salaries which have stayed at an average of 1 million zlotys a
month (= 600 French francs). What is the solution?

J.G. - The solution comes through patience. Right now,
there is no expressway toward prosperity, and the people are
motivated to build the future. The government looks for the

means by establishing a free-market economy along with privatization.

R.L. - This austere politic, when will it bear its first fruits?

J.G. - We hope for the first concrete amelioration in 1991. But, let's be realistic, we will have to count on objective obstacles from the outside. The Gulf war has caused breaches of contracts which delay us. The unification of Germany deprives us of the closest market: East Germany; and we cannot very well count on our eastern neighbor, whose economy is actually in chaos.

R.L. - For more than 20 years, during 15 of my trips to Poland, I have seen a constant rise in faith. Elsewhere, this fervor is decreasing. I was afraid it would be the same under Gierek, whose plan was to put faith to sleep by prosperity (as had been tried in Spain). But that negative prognostic did not come through. Faith remained and has not ceased to grow deeper until the election of the Pope and beyond...Is it still the case?

J.G. - Yes.

J.G. - Maybe in the large towns where it has fallen from 25 to 30%, but it is a small decrease. In the country and small towns, the rate is a lot higher: 50, 70% and more...

R.L. - Under Marxism, many agnostics went to mass because it was the only way to protest against the regime. You have obviously lost these customers: they have no more reason to come...On another point, the western press (including the Catholic press) criticized the decision that brings back religious teaching in school. It has been said that this decision was taken against the majority?

J.G. - No, the approval was massive.

R.L. - It was in fact the tradition of your country, up to the Marxist regime. After getting rid of religious teaching upon his arrival to power, he had to bring it back, during the 50's. A mother told me: "At first I was against it, for practical reasons: teaching in the school takes the children away from the parish and the Church. It may weaken religious formation. But now, I agree and that saves me a lot of time. I do not have to take my children to catechism anymore."

J.G. - Recently I was seeing the parish priest of a town of 20 000 people, only two students asked not to have religious education. They did it freely and the school gave them an education conforming to their convictions during that time.

R.L. - Where does the false news that presents Polish education so negatively come from? It has been said that it came from the Communists, who kept their post in the administration.

J.G. - It can come from non-Communist atheists. Where religious education in school is concerned, Orthodox and Protestants are happy with this solution.

R.L. - You proposed it in co-ordination with them?

J.G. - No, but the demand was done by all the confessions which also have their religious education; and it has always been agreed that the new regime is established with all respect for the conscience and opinions of each person.

R.L. - Walesa has just proposed his candidacy for president. What are his chances?

J.G. - I can give you one objective response: in the polls published this morning (March 22) in the Gazeta Swiateczna ("Gazette of the voters": he has it in his hand), Mazowiecki is in 2nd position with 70% (4 points lower than in June), and

Walesa is in 3rd position with 64%, that is a 10% increase since June; the number of opponents has fallen 20 to 14% for him and has gone up 6 to 8% for Mazowiecki.

R.L. - Mazowiecki and Walesa are number 2 and 3, but who is *number one* in that poll?

The Cardinal shows me the newspaper: it is him, with 80%, and 3% of opponents only. (We do not know how, since then, Walesa has outdone Mazowiecki, and has won the Presidency, with the conviction that was it was his mission. The Cardinal remains in first place, but all have gone down with the austerity; he, by 70%.)

R.L. - A few years ago, during the state of siege, you were told you were losing popularity, as opposed to Wyszynski, whose prestige has remained number one in permanence. You are back to the top. This position in the polls must facilitate the role of referee you still have in cardinal Wyszynski's wake, this giant, of whom you were the principal collaborator. The international press has talked a lot about your invitation to the leaders of Poland, on September 28, 1990: General-President Jaruzelski, the Prime Minister, Mazowiecki, Walesa, current-candidate and the two Presidents of the Senate and the Chamber: Stelmachowski and Korakiwicz. In France, it would be unthinkable to have the president of the Episcopal Conference invite all the supreme authorities of the country in such a way. Do we still remember that here the Primate of Poland was the Interrex: the Regent between the reigns... But I think the guests were more numerous. How did it go?

J.G. - I received the five of them from lunch until 4 o'clock in the afternoon. Twenty-eight more then came, and we talked until 8: 30. I kept for dinner the 5 guests from lunch.

R.L. - This invitation, was it difficult to make them accept it?

J.G. - Not at all. The only regrets are with those... who were not invited. But it was impossible to invite everybody all the way to the small parties, if we wanted that informal exchange to be fruitful.

R.L. - At what time did you finish?

J.G. - At 9:30.

R.L. - Some speak of a decline in vocations in Poland?

J.G. - Instead I see a stability. There were 73 entries in the seminar in Varsovie, last October. Very rare are the years in which they went up to 80. In the large seminary, there are 333. To that you can add the religious institutes that offer courses: 72 and the neo-catechumen:38. That makes it above 400.

R.L. - How is the family? In most western countries, the current evolution erodes it in a worrying way. The number of marriages, religious as well as civil, has decreased considerably during the past few years, not only in France, but also in Italy, and Poland seems affected by this period phenomenon, despite the familial pastoral which was reinforced by John-Paul II.

J.G. - At home, almost all of the weddings are legalized. Those who divorce usually re-register their civil marriage.

R.L. - What about cohabitation?

J.G. - Very rare here.

R.L - Divorces?

J.G - People say it is decreasing.

R.L. - Has alcoholism gone down?

J.G. - That is not so evident.

R.L. - People also talk about drugs, and AIDS.

J.G. - The Camilliens are taking care of it.

R.L. - You are one of the rare countries where catechism give a true instruction and Christian formation. It was the labor of the parishes. How will we find a qualified personnel from this transfer to the school?

J.G. - We have formed 100'0 more catechist this year. We already have 1500 of them in 1989, and more than 2000 in 1990.

R.L. - Will that be enough for religious instruction in all the schools?

J.G. - YES.

R.L. - Now that the instruction is transferred to the schools, what do you do with your catechism rooms?

J.G. - In many cases, we loan them to the schools.

R.L. - A good co-ordination reigns in Poland, more than the western press leads one to suspect.

R.L. - Before you leave us, do you have a message for France?

The Cardinal gives an evasive gesture as if to say: I have neither lessons to give nor answers:

J.G. - We are mostly grateful for what France has done for us: your food and economical aide is very useful during this transition, and the numerous grants which were given to us. I have in permanence about ten seminarists and 25 priests in France.

In fact, it is from France that large quantities of initiatives, mostly private, come from. The trucks full of food and pharmaceutical products help to solve the gravest problem right now: the survival of a people whose minimum salary is 368 000 zlots a month: 240 francs. Even if you reach the average salary, around 600 francs, it takes two salaries for a family to make it... with difficulty. The truth on the price has gotten rid of the lines in the stores but that only benefits those who can buy. A person who is in that case told me:

-With my large salary I had big problems with food, because my professional work did not allow me to stay in line for hours. Now that the price have gone up 10 times and more, I do not feel disadvantaged anymore.

R.L. - Allow me one last question: the press gave, last year, alarming news about your health and your surgery. Looking at you, one does not see it.

J.G. - I feel better than before.

The Cardinal gives me the impression of a calm, and available, man, present for all, welcoming all people and all information, with rapid and advised reactions. He is a man of communication and decision. His predecessor was a founder. After being his principal collaborator, Cardinal Glemp is the providential referee in a new situation. Beyond the never ending fight against oppression, the problem now is invention, creativity, co-organization for the solution of a formidable backlog. It is not easy, because the sacred union of all the Polish in front of Russo-Marxist oppression suddenly finds itself in front of the emptiness of the future. They are now back to their free initiatives and responsibilities. The divergences are unavoidable. Walesa seems to have been afraid that his collaborator Mazowiecki, who became his rival, would give too many pledges to the liberal non Catholic intelligentsia, and would become the Trojan Horse of a new anti-clericalism or freemasonry, in full expansion in the eastern countries. This opposition of the two winners of Communism has shocked. The life and building of a people do not happen without tensions. Luckily, they are supported by the fullness of faith, admirably formed during half a century of heroism.

Poland was the no.1 catalyst for liberations in the East (see above, p.3-10). The oppressed of yesterday have taken power democratically, thus taking on responsibilities, in conditions as difficult as in Romania and the USSR, which are not even making it on the economic level. It is a time of tensions. At the threshold of the presidential elections, I took stock with the Primate of Poland, Cardinal Glemp; and I give as an epilogue the archives of the prayer of heroic times.

2

The prayers of the martyred Poland

Walesa's two prayers

At the time of his early triumphs, Lech Walesa came to Czestochowa as the leader of the free syndicate that had been accepted through a great fight. He incorporates his effort to the Consecration of Poland, by Cardinal-Primate Wyszynski.

1. Recognition at the time of triumph

Holy Virgin, I come to you with all the simplicity of my heart, to tell you: I put myself in your hands, I give myself to you entirely. After the Holy-Father John-Paul II, I repeat: In you is my trust.

On this day, I put my heart in your hands. the heart of my heart in the town of Gdansk. I put down at your feet its coat of arms as a sign of gratefulness, for all you have done for this town and all over the literal, for our Country and for the Church.

One more time, assuming a great responsibility for the fate of our country, after the Cardinal Primate, I repeat: I have put everything on the Blessed Virgin.

Holy Virgin, it is not only me I entrust in you, but also all of Poland, the Church that is in Poland and everything Poland represents. I entrust all our country lives from today: all its worries, all its experiences, all its sufferings, as well as all its great hopes for a better future.

I especially entrust to you maternal cares the independent and autonomous syndicates of Solidarity. Guide them, Holy Mother, protects their rights, to those who assume the workers interest and defend their right and dignity.

Take our country under your protection, I implore you: That Poland becomes a home for men, a home for God's children, that justice, liberty, peace, love and solidarity triumph.

Finally (...), Holy Mother, guide me. I want to be in your hands an instrument to the service of my country, of the Church and the other men. Turn your merciful glance especially to the workers and the farmers of Gdansk and all the other countries. Protect them and strengthen their will as well as their heart in this fight for the legitimate rights of the country and the Church in Poland. Amen[1].

–Lech Walesa, October 1980

2. Renunciation and trust at the time of failure
Walesa's prayer in prison

Incarcerated in 1981, after the dissolution of *Solidarity*, Walesa ask for the power to forgive. His consecration reaches here distressing depths. May the President keep his breath:

Holy Mother, I have lost my insignia

Of the Holy Virgin of Czestochowa

Weeping in the December snow.

From the depths of my heart it has fallen,

Accompanied by the hurt inflicted upon us.

186

It penetrated all the way to my soul.

That is where I find You,

That is where my battered and betrayed country rejoins You.

That is where I will keep vigil in silence.

And I will continue.

Do you hear? Millions of heart beat in me.

By making this appeal, as long as we live.

Holy Mother, my Mother,

Mother of our Mother-Country,

Give us the strength to support our fate

Till the end,

May your flame guide us toward liberty and truth.

And forgive those who offend us

When we cannot anymore[2].

187

Polish litany at the time of distress (1982)

At the time of the State of Siege and the repressions, here are the litanies which circulated in *Solidarity*'s circles: they reveal the secret of a victorious patience:

Mother of the fools

Mother of the betrayed ones

Mother of the men arrested in the night

Mother of the interned ones

Mother of the imprisoned ones

Mother of the beaten up ones

Mother of the terrified ones

Mother of the murdered ones

Mother of the coal miners

Mother of the workers of ship yards

Mother of the workers

Mother of the students

Mother of the sentenced innocents

Mother of those who cannot lie

Mother of those who cannot buy

Mother of those who cannot be broken

Mother of the desperate ones

Mother of the orphans

grant us the gift of life

in truth and freedom. Amen![3]

EPILOGUE

The opening of the Iron Wall(dictatorial citadell of atheism) to democracy, liberty, and God is a great event of the 20h century, providing the hope for John-Paul II's long-time prophecy of a unified Europe. This can seem utopic, because nothing is sure... on many levels!

In the East, the spectacular change that sprang up with a rapidity stupefying at first can only end up in order, not in chaos. However, it is difficult to change too many things at once without falling into disorder and disintegration. This was the drama of the Post-Council, around May 68, and an inevitable problem for Gorbachev who did not solve it. He seems to be reduced to slow the disintegration by slowing progress, for lack of another viable solution, and to fall back on the old ways of Communism to maintain the apparent order.

On the other hand, the good news which was opening the way to a Unified Europe from the Atlantic to the Urals has been quickly tarnished, not only by this return backwards, but also by the birth of another hearth of war where antagonism remains latent - Islam against Israel and against the West tied to the United States. The sound of bombs and the obscure images of blood and death exacerbates a fanaticism without precedent. The USSR itself suffers from a grave crisis glasnost has loosened the tongues, the press and hope, brilliantly in euphoria. But the restructuring of perestroika remains a failure with a worrisome lack of power. Professor Yves has worries because of the irreformable nature of the Marxist system. Finally, the opening to western values: democracy, spirit of enterprise, freedom, including religious, comes with an indistinct opening to the vice of the capitalist civilization - erotism, rock and substitutes, and the unilateral cult of profit and consumerism.

Christianity which has played a large role in freeing glasnost, continues her urgent mission of inspiring not only moral order, the objective cult of rightiousness, patience and perseverance, but also the gift of oneself and the prophetic burst toward a world in which love fulfills, from a world in which desire and frenzy of having, knowing and power dominate. The issue of evolution that is trying to understand itself, not without idealism and generosity, could not be materialistic. If it were a matter of going from Marxist theoretical materialism, the advantage would be small and debatable. The future will be spiritual and Christian, or will not be. The official Church works well to establish peaceful, ecumenical, cooperative relations with other countries, and with the non-Christian religions. These negotiations are necessary and directed wisely. But that is only the surface. Everything must be renewed from the inside, from the divine source, being understood that God is Love. The secret of the future is that it will be a future with God, or will not be. There is no future for a plant without its nourishing root.

Life will be the strongest. God will be the strongest.

Russia Father Polocin

1. So then because thou art lukewarm, and neither cold nor hot, I will spew thee out of my mouth." (Rev. 3:16)

Page 63 *The Russian feminist movement, Maria*

2. Tatiana GORITCHEVA, "Delivered from the tears of Eve, rejoice!" in *Femmes et Russie*, 1980, by the collective writing of the Almanac, Paris, Editions des Femmes, 1980, pp. 27-34. T.G. belongs to the Christian feminist movement which founded, in 1980, the movement and journal *Maria*, under Mary's patronage.

Page 65

3. Svetlana SANOVA, *A friend's answer to "Delivered from the tears of Eve, rejoice!"*, in *Russian women, by women of Leningrad and other towns*, ib., 1980, pp. 97-110.

Page 104 *Apparitions in Ukraine*

1. Fayard 1989, pp. 133-138.

2. In Ukrainian, some transcribe Hrushiv, because G is guttural. The English prefer *sh* to *ch*, which is pronounced *tch* in their language.

page 157 *Romania: Anton Gotia*

1. I met Anton and Marie Emmanuelle's family in their apartment in a new neighborhood. I saw their children - Stefan Anton, 18 years old, who intends to take up agronomy, Andren Josif, 16 years old, who seems to be

tending towards Literature, as is Dominica Maria, 15 years old, Anna Maria, 13 years old, is very attracted to Mother Teresa. The youngest, Ioan Patricio, is 12 years old.

Page 186   *The prayers of the martyred Poland*

1. Polish source.

   The weekly *Argumenty*, organ of the *Association of the secular culture*, echoed by *Tribuna Ludu (The people's tribune*, organ of the Polish Communist Party), published an article entitled *"The Political Madonna"*. The theme is that she is used to "create a domination of the Church over the Socialist State". The article stigmatizes "the massive wearing of images of the Blessed Virgin on more or less clean clothes", the "banners on which Madonnas wearing the Polish crown are weaved". "The outlawed union," the article specifies, "appropriated with the agreement or at least without protestation by the Church, the symbols of the Blessed Virgin linked, of course, to the white and red (national) colors and to Anti-Communism."

   Walesa views the problem from another angle. Questioned about mass and regular communion, he answered; "It is the source of my strength. Without them, my head would explode. I consider the Blessed Virgin as the Queen of Poland, and I often pray to her."

Page 187

2. Polish source.

Page 189

3. In *Pray*, October 1, 1982, p. 18.

Telephone Marketing